WHEN I
CAME TO DIE

When I Came to Die

PROCESS AND PROPHECY
IN THOREAU'S
VISION OF DYING

Audrey Raden

University of Massachusetts Press
Amherst and Boston

Copyright © 2017 by University of Massachusetts Press
All rights reserved
Printed in the United States of America

ISBN 978-1-62534-240-9 (paper); 239-3 (hardcover)

Designed by Jack Harrison
Set in Adobe Garamond Pro
Printed and bound by The Maple-Vail Book Manufacturing Group

Cover design by Jack Harrison
Cover art: Digitally altered photo of autumn leaves
© Abdul Sami Haqqani | Dreamstime.

Library of Congress Cataloging-in-Publication Data
A catalog record for this book is available from the Library of Congress.

British Library Cataloguing-in-Publication Data
A catalog record for this book is available from the British Library.

I went to the woods because I wished to live deliberately, to front only the essential facts of life, and see if I could not learn what it had to teach, and not, when I came to die, discover that I had not lived.

—HENRY DAVID THOREAU, *Walden*

Contents

Preface

This book began its life in May 2002. Early in that month, I traveled alone for the first time to Concord, Massachusetts, in time for the anniversary of Thoreau's death. I sniffed the last of the apple blossoms, walked to Walden Pond and Sleepy Hollow Cemetery, and in general enjoyed being a pilgrim of transcendentalism. Fortunately, the last day of my trip was rainy, so that I got to spend the entire day in the Concord Free Public Library. I looked at the paintings, busts, and plaques, stared reverently at Daniel Chester French's sculpture of Emerson, and then sat down to write.

Thoreau's late essays had inspired me to write about his approach to the process of dying. I have always been drawn to writings about the end of life (no doubt because of all the Victorian novels I have read), and I was struck by the similarity of the imagery that Thoreau used to describe both the death of John Brown and the death of the year. The fact that he wrote about them so close to his own death piqued my imagination further. As I began my research, I discovered that no one had ever written a full-length study on Thoreau and dying. In fact, very few articles even discussed it. A book needed to be written.

My first thanks must go to Sarah Lazarus and Ken Lazarus, the owners of the lovely Yellow House on Main Street in Concord, where Thoreau lived for the last twelve years of his life and where he died. As I was close to finishing this book in January 2013, they graciously gave me, a stranger, a tour, allowed me to see his attic study and the front parlor where he died. This visit helped my work immensely.

I thank David Reynolds, my intellectual mentor at the City University of New York's graduate school, who never gave up on my endeavors, even when I was ready to give up on them myself; as well as Robert A. Gross, who began as an outside reader and became a dear friend. It was he who introduced my manuscript to the University of Massachusetts Press. I am grateful to my editors at the press, Clark Dougan, Matt Becker, and Carol Betsch, Karen Fisk, and my copyeditor, Dawn Potter, who were infinitely patient with me. I also thank my first reader, Jeffrey Berman, for his kind encouragement and my anonymous second reader, who helped me refine my draft into a book.

My research benefited from the patient assistance of Leslie Perrin Wilson, the Special Collections curator at the Concord Free Public Library and her staff assistant, Constance Minoli-Skocay; Jeffrey Cramer, curator of the Thoreau Institute in Lincoln, Massachusetts; and David F. Wood, curator of the Concord Museum. The faculty and staff of New York Theological Seminary made it possible for me to finish this book while completing a master's degree in divinity. Special thanks go to Dale Irvin, Jin Hee Han, Ava Carroll, Jerry Reisig, Jill Schaeffer, and Lillian Rodriguez.

I am grateful for the insights, guidance, and good fellowship of the members of the Thoreau and Emerson societies, particularly Phyllis Cole, Robert Hudspeth, the late Bradley P. Dean, the late Edmund Schofield, Michael Schliefer, Mike Frederick, Laura Dassow Walls, Sandra Herbert Petrolionus, Kevin Van Anglan, John Matteson, Richard Smith, Peter Alden, Dianne McConville Weiss, and Victor Curran. In addition, as Emerson said of Thoreau, my dear friends "never faltered," and their brilliance and encouragement have been a pleasure and a gift: Marvin Lifschitz, Patrick Martin, Victoria Wolfson, Louis Asekoff, Greg Wilson, Vickie Wilson, Rachel Ihara, Jaime Cleland, Vincent Sanchez, Mitchell Lichtenstein, Miguel Arisa, Carter Johnson, Jonathan Golby, David Kaplan, Marilyn Mudry, Gregory Burch, and especially my beloved editorial elves and writing partners Jenny Weiss, T. Meyerhoff, and Cori L. Gabbard.

I also thank my family, my kitty muse Increase, and especially "My Dear and Loving Husband" John Eiche:

> *If ever two were one, then surely we.*
> *If ever man were loved by wife, then thee:*
> *If ever wife were happy in a man,*
> *Compare with me ye women if you can.*

WHEN I
CAME TO DIE

INTRODUCTION

Anticipation as Prophecy

It is not important that [a man] should mature as an apple-tree
or oak. Shall he turn his spring into summer?

—HENRY DAVID THOREAU, *Walden*

I

Nature is always dying; Henry David Thoreau knew this and spent his
entire life saying good-bye. Of course, he knew that nature is also always
living; but beautifully and paradoxically, he was able to portray dying as
the truest form of living. Likewise, though this book is ostensibly about the
theme of dying in Thoreau's writings, it focuses on a particular transition—
the nontemporal, nonspatial existence between two states that is neither
one nor the other. For Thoreau, that state exists primarily in the process of
dying. Dying is continual and integral to creation. To be dead is to step out
of the innocent cycles of nature, whereas to be dying—"really dying," as he
writes in *Walden*—is to be continually participating in nature.[1]

One cannot fairly call Thoreau death-obsessed, for he lived in a culture that was deeply invested in death and in dying well. In his vast and
brilliant study *The Hour of Our Death*, Philippe Ariès posits that in the
nineteenth century, as interest in a traditional notion of salvation began
to fade, emphasis shifted to the actual moment of death, when the soul
parted from the body and the dying person separated from loved ones.
In a "beautiful death," Ariès explains, the character of the dying person is
reflected in the holiness of his or her dying.[2] One cannot underestimate
the importance of dying beautifully to mid-nineteenth-century Americans. Jeremy Taylor's *Holy Dying* (1876), a step-by-step manual on how to

die with resignation, cheerfulness, and hope, was much more popular than his earlier *Holy Living*.[3]

This idea of the beautiful death was familiar to both the Emerson and the Thoreau families. After Thoreau's brother John died agonizingly of lockjaw in January 1842, Ralph Waldo Emerson's wife Lidian wrote to her sister Lucy Jackson Brown: "It's a beautiful fate that has been granted him and I think he was worthy of it." Later in the month, still thinking about John's death, she wrote to her sister again: "During the hour in which he died, he looked at Henry with a transcendent smile full of heaven . . . and Henry found himself returning it and this was the last communication that passed between them."[4] In a similar vein, when Thoreau himself died of consumption twenty years later, his sister Sophia wrote to his friend Daniel Ricketson that something "beautiful" had happened.[5] Such epistolary recordings of deathbed scenes were common in the antebellum period.

In his classic essay "Death in the Popular Mind of Pre–Civil War America," Lewis O. Saum writes, "The acme of privilege came in witnessing a 'triumphant' death. In the abstract, one encounters the contention that 'holy dying' represented the logical finality of 'holy living.'"[6] The bulk of his fascinating essay is comprised of excerpts from letters written to and from Americans who had moved west that describe the deathbed scenes of loved ones and answer earnest questions about the quality of those deaths. Yet both Saum and, to a certain extent, Ariès assume that records of such scenes were important mostly to the uneducated, whom Saum calls the "unlettered."[7] In fact, however, much of what we know about Thoreau's dying was recorded by his fellow transcendentalists, especially in letters written by the well-educated Sophia.

Dying in the antebellum United States was far different from dying in contemporary America. Today more than 70 percent of Americans die in hospitals, but in Thoreau's time the vast majority died at home. The dying were cared for by their families and neighbors, and after death their bodies were washed and prepared for burial at home. Because embalming did not become standard practice until the Civil War, when large numbers of men died far away from their homes, funerals took place soon after death.

Dying was also more frequent in the antebellum period: life expectancy was shorter, childhood diseases were often fatal, and many infants and women died during childbirth. The temporal and spatial nearness of death and dying made them everyday realities, and their ubiquity greatly influenced popular literature, music, and art. In her essay "Reclaiming Sentimental Literature," the literary historian Joanne Dobson suggests a link between the worldview of the sentimental narrative and the pervasive cultural experience of death and dying: "The sentimental crisis of consciousness is not so much an anxiety regarding the ultimate nonbeing of the self as it is a certain knowledge of inevitable separation—whether temporal or eternal—from the others who constitute the meaning of one's life."[8]

In his writings, Thoreau meshed his culture's fascination with dying, his transcendental fascination with and rejection of human time (what he called "railroad time"), his repugnance at the physicality of death, his lifelong disgust for graves and stone monuments, his mysticism, and his attention to the natural world, in which dying is the ultimate transition state. Throughout his life, he wrestled with these associations, writing about death as putrefaction, scorning the need for meaningless and costly memorials, and lamenting wasted lives. Notably, his late political essay, "A Plea for Captain John Brown," reiterates that people who do not live in the true sense cannot die in the natural sense. Yet even his early writings exhibit this sentiment. In the earliest draft of *Walden's* "Economy" chapter, he writes, "Why should [farmers] eat their sixty acres, when man is condemned to eat his peck of dirt? Why should they begin digging their graves as soon as they are born?"[9] On March 12, 1842, two months after his brother's death but four years before he began drafting *Walden,* he wrote in his Journal: "To die is not to *begin* to die—and *continue*—it is not a state of continuance but of transientness—but to live is a condition of continuance and does not mean to be born merely—There is no continuance of death—it is a transient phenomenon—Nature presents nothing in a state of death."[10]

In Thoreau's memory, in his flute playing, and especially in his writing, his brother was always living. Yet he was also always dying. People in the nineteenth century reserved the word *closure* for doors and boxes, not for grieving. Thus, though Thoreau saw death as grotesque, he saw dying as an aspect of the Romantic sublime—powerful and not completely knowable—and it formed a core of the mysticism that influenced his own experience of dying. For Thoreau, dying was a state of ecstasy similar to what he had felt in nature as a young man and that he had continued to experience less often but with the same intensity as he aged. Even though he was dying away from the woods and in his mother's parlor, he felt ecstasy because the experience was a purely natural state. Thoreau believed that everything exists in a state of transition and that thought is the highest form of action. Dying, too, they saw as a transitional action. By working too hard to stay alive, people step out of nature and thus become more dead.

A year after Thoreau's death, while reading his friend's enormous Journal, Emerson wrote in his own, "In reading him, I find the same thought, the same spirit that is in me, but he takes it a step beyond, & illustrates by excellent images that which I would have conveyed in a sleepy generality."[11] This famous passage could easily be misinterpreted as " 'Self-Reliance'— Emerson wrote about it; Thoreau lived it!" Yet the passage has nothing to do with how Thoreau lived: it is about Thoreau's writing and thinking, which are as extravagant as his physical life was simple, pure, and abstemious. One important idea that he borrowed from Emerson's work is the concept of transition. In the essay "Self-Reliance," Emerson declares, "Life only avails, not the having lived. Power ceases in the moment of repose; it resides in the moment of transition from a past state to a new state."[12] Similarly, in *Walden,* Thoreau writes, "In any hour of the day or night, I have been anxious to improve the nick of time . . . to stand on the meeting of two eternities, the past and the future, which is precisely the present moment."[13] Because the actual present is always passing away, it never exists in perceivable time. Therefore, to live in the eternal present, one must step away from linear time into a space in which one can perceive the present by experiencing it prospectively. As in a painting, a moment in time can only be re-created and represented. Thoreau subtly makes this spatial distinction by choosing the preposition "on" rather than "in." At the "meeting of two eternities," there is no future or past. The actual cessation of life is therefore nearly impossible to experience: it is an instantaneous eternity that exists between living and dying.

Like Thoreau, Emerson returns again and again to the idea of transition states, most beautifully in his essay "Experience," which repeats "Everything good is on the highway" twice in a single paragraph.[14] This highway doesn't exist in any real sense but is part of the ideality that is a theme of the essay. In Emerson's terms, an imaginary road is preferable for travel. One does not have to imagine a destination but can simply move in the eternal moment.

Emerson's highway of the mind is one of his "sleepy generalities," which Thoreau "takes . . . a step beyond & illustrates with excellent images." Thoreau's lecture-essay "Walking," considers an actual physical road that, like Emerson's highway, goes nowhere and everywhere. Partway into the piece, Thoreau inserts a seemingly comic poem, "The Old Marlborough Road," "because I presume there are one or two such roads in every town." Nearly two pages long, the poem's narrow but not completely straight lines resemble the shape of a road, and its content encapsulates the author's thinking. Thoreau begins by expressing his contempt for burgeoning antebellum capitalism, telling us the toll road was abandoned because it was no longer making money and alluding to an unsuccessful treasure hunt in the neighborhood. Later in the poem, he mentions the "Cenotaphs of towns"—the stone guideposts abandoned by towns that have built newer, more efficient roads. Thus, the road represents a return to the primitive.[15]

Thoreau sparsely populates the road with a set of representative real-life characters from the Concord area. Among them is the hunter Elisha Dugan (historical records tell us he was an African American), who, like the Canadian woodchopper, a character in *Walden,* spends his days trapping and eating small animals—continuing to live as his victims continue to die. Although Thoreau treats Dugan comically—"Where life is sweetest / He constantly eateth"—readers catch an air of Thoreau himself at Walden Pond, who also lived alone and, metaphorically at least, desired to "suck all the marrow out of life."[16] Thoreau juxtaposes Dugan with Elijah Wood, a successful Concord landowner and boot manufacturer. (Notice their first names: the greatest Old Testament prophet and his successor.)[17] Thus, Thoreau not only puts Dugan on equal footing with Wood but also mythologizes him, just as he does with the vanished and vanishing fishermen he describes in *A Week on the Concord and Merrimack Rivers,* the long-dead inhabitants of Walden Woods and the Irish who built the railroad in *Walden,* the loggers and Indian guides in *The Maine Woods,* the wreckers and lighthouse keepers in *Cape Cod,* and his own solitary self.

The poem's opening lines, "When the spring stirs my blood / With the instinct to travel," paraphrase the opening lines of Geoffrey Chaucer's *The Canterbury Tales,* which Thoreau quotes at the beginning of the essay. Moreover, like Chaucer's poem, Thoreau's is full of Christian allusions, and he characterizes his daily walk as both a holy quest and a pilgrimage. After noting that no one important uses the old road, he nonetheless declares,

"It's a living way / As the Christians say." To understand this couplet, we must recall his distaste for stone monuments, many of which line this old road. (As he writes in *A Week on the Concord and Merrimack Rivers*, "most of the stone a nation hammers goes toward its tomb only. It buries itself alive.")[18] How can the road be "a living way" if it is mostly deserted and lined with weathered tombstones? Unlike the dead, who can be re-created in imagination as living or dying, the crumbling stones have no relation to the once-living and, in Thoreau's view, are a profanation of them. Yet "the living way" of an older Christianity, the Congregationalism of the transcendentalists' elderly relatives, was a constant movement toward perfection, much like John Bunyan's allegory in *The Pilgrim's Progress*. This tradition accepted that perfection could be achieved only by dying from this life into a holier one, where our sins would fall from our backs and we would reunite with God. In Thoreau's vision, process can lead us toward a prelapsarian reunification with nature. Although antebellum New England Unitarianism posited that human perfectibility was achievable in this life through rational virtue, Thoreau believed that this attitude led to self-satisfaction and to lives devoted to commerce and status, which progressed only to meaninglessness, quiet desperation, and blank tombstones.

The railroad that had brought Thoreau to the town lyceum to deliver this lecture was changing the landscape of New England. By including the poem within that essay, he was able to suggest that something is lost when the old roads are abandoned to make room for such efficiency. The landscape that Thoreau and his listeners remembered from their childhoods would soon vanish altogether. But did they cease to exist? How are humans related to the dead past? As the poem says, "one or two" listeners or readers may still follow the old abandoned roads with their feet and their minds. The concluding lines, "You may go round the world / By the old Marlborough Road,"[19] heightens the circularity of the essay and emphasizes the cycle of life and death, in which dying embraces all living.

The Marlborough Road was not the only semi-abandoned road in the Concord area to capture Thoreau's imagination. On September 24, 1859, he wrote in his Journal:

Road—that old Carlisle one—that leaves towns behind; where you do not carry a watch, nor remember the proprietor; where the proprietor is the only trespasser,—looking after *his* apples!—the only one who mistakes his calling there, whose title is not good; where fifty may be a-barberrying and you do not see one. It is an endless succession of glades where the barberries grow thickest, successive yards amid the barberry bushes where you do not see out. There I see Melvin and the robins, and many a nut-brown maid sashaying to the barberry bushes in hoops and crinoline, and none of them see me. The world-surrounding hoop! faery rings! Oh, the jolly cooper's trade it is the best of any! Carried to the furthest isles where civilized man penetrates. This is the girdle they've put round the world! Saturn or Satan set the example. Large and small hogsheads, barrels, kegs, worn by misses that go to the lone school house in the Pinkham Notch. The lonely horse in its pasture is glad to see company, comes forward to be noticed and takes an apple from your hand. Others are called great roads, but this is greater than they all. The road is not only laid out, offered to walkers, not *accepted* by the town and the traveling world. To be represented as a dotted line on charts, or drawn in lime-juice, undiscoverable to the uninitiated, to be held to a warm imagination. No guide-boards indicate it. No odometer would indicate the miles a wagon had run there. Rocks which the Druids *might* have raised—if they could. There I go searching for malic acid of the right quality, with my tests. The process is simple. Place the fruit between your jaws and then endeavor to make your teeth meet. The very earth contains it. The Easterbrooks Country contains malic acid.[20]

Though very different from the neat couplets of "The Old Marlborough Road," this almost hallucinatory association of images shares the poem's theme of circularity. As the scholar Randall Conrad has noted, most of the objects mentioned are round: apples, barberries, hoops and crinolines, the jolly cooper, faery rings, the earth's girdle, hogsheads, kegs, barrels, the rings of Saturn, and the earth itself. Moreover, "with these two words, 'faery rings,' Thoreau's circles acquire more connotations: magic, punishment, blindness. We remember that along the Old Carlisle Road, the successive 'yards' are bounded by barberry bushes. *Those* are the fairy rings. We are the people who can't see out—or the ones who can't see in." This mystery is also present in "The Old Marlborough Road," where Thoreau hints at the road's invisible life. Writing of the Journal entry, Conrad says, "Thoreau designates 'a warm imagination' rather than a physical fire as the heat source. Imagination allows us to see—and read—what is invisible. Our experience on the Old Carlisle Road requires imagination, which gives the road its true value."[21] Just as Thoreau imaginatively re-creates the dead on the Old Marlborough Road, he brings to mind the long dead by introducing ancient imagery into the Journal passage: "faery rings," "Druids," "a nut-brown maid," a "jolly cooper."

Thoreau "sees Melvin, and the robins, and many a nut-brown maid" on the Carlisle Road. Like Elisha Dugan, Melvin is a hunter and border character. Thoreau naturalizes Melvin, as well as the maids, by juxtaposing them with the robin. Conrad notes that calling the maids "nut-brown" implies ripeness. Hunting and gathering barberries and apples suggest autumn, one of the richest seasons, when the year culminates and begins to die. The circularity that graces the Old Carlisle Road, like the Old Marlborough Road, implies both eternity and a complete life cycle. Thoreau saunters on these old roads to leave worldliness behind. According to Conrad, he "uses 'worldly' . . . not in our contemporary sense of 'sophisticated,' but in a traditional religious sense referring to the material world, the realm of all things profane, as opposed to the spiritual realm."[22] To step away from the old sense of worldliness on the old roads, to make the "proprietor" unimportant, is to escape the bounds of time and space. Thoreau reveals the true proprietor as nature, which to him is always female.

Consideration of this Thoreauvian circularity is an element of just one approach to Thoreau studies rather than a holistic view of the writer's life and work. Many scholars talk about the three Thoreaus: the naturalist and proto-ecologist, the political activist and abolitionist, and the prose stylist and philosopher.[23] To his earliest readers, he was Thoreau the naturalist, and that version of his character has become popularized in the past few decades alongside the development of ecocriticism. Lawrence Buell's *The Environmental Imagination* and Laura Dassow Walls's *Seeing New Worlds* are important considerations of Thoreau the naturalist.[24] In *John Brown, Abolitionist,* David S. Reynolds offers a detailed reading of Thoreau the abolitionist, encouraging us to reread Thoreau's political writings in a twenty-first-century context.[25] Beginning with Sherman Paul's *The Shores of America,* now more than fifty years old, there have been many wonderful books about Thoreau's prose and philosophy, particularly, in recent years, his extraordinary Journal.[26]

In this book, I, too, propose a triune Thoreau, encapsulated in his three approaches to dying: the sentimental or domestic, the heroic, and the physical and mystical. My approach will be primarily thematic rather than chronological, as Thoreau's ideas about dying did not change much over the course of his life, though he found new ways to express them as a writer. Nonetheless, there is a temporal aspect to the book, which opens

and closes with two biographical chapters: the first on the death of Thoreau's beloved brother John, the last on his own death twenty years later.
Chapters 2 through 4, though mainly analytical, also discuss aspects of his
life and his personal sensibilities.

While separating his three approaches is a necessary rhetorical device,
there was great fluidity among them, both in his writing and thinking and
in the intellectual and popular culture of the time. For example, the idea of
the seed reappears frequently in his work, from his earliest Journal entries
to the end of his life, and it was also a sentimental trope of the era. Thoreau
plays on the common idea that many annual plants, like the tender mothers of the nineteenth-century imagination, die so that their children, their
seeds, may live. Seeds travel heroically, by wind or animal, to wherever
they are dropped, where they rot, feed animals, or grow into a new life for
another generation. With similar stoicism, fruits and leaves joyfully and
beautifully lay down their lives for the sake of the earth. As Thoreau says
in several places, he has "faith in a seed."[27] Faith implies belief in a mystery.
A seed is both itself and not itself, for an acorn holds, as Emerson says, an
entire oak forest.[28] In this sense, tender nurturance leads to stoic denial of
self and from there to transformation.

Chapter 1 briefly discusses the history of consumption, or tuberculosis,
in New England, especially in the Emerson and Thoreau families. It also
considers the Thoreau brothers' relationship, including their dual courtship of Ellen Sewall and the tension and guilt Thoreau may have felt in
leaving his own home for the Emersons'. The chapter's primary textual
focus is a close reading of *A Week on the Concord and Merrimack Rivers* in
terms of prophetic anticipation and universal dying in nature.

Chapter 2 concentrates on Thoreau's domestic relationship to the natural world as revealed in *Walden* and his Journal. It also examines the letters
he exchanged with his family and the Emersons. I discuss recent contemporary criticism about men and sentimental culture and question the long-
held assumption that nineteenth-century men and women functioned in
separate spheres. Thoreau may have grumbled that the local library's most
popular book was Susan Warner's *The Wide, Wide World,* but there are
striking similarities between Thoreau and his sentimental contemporaries,
particularly Harriet Beecher Stowe, who shared his concerns about abolition and forest preservation. The chapter speculatively considers the Christian orientation of his writings and talks about the nostalgia for boyhood

that informs so much of his work and influenced his behavior and choices as an adult.

Chapter 3 discusses Thoreau's heroic approach to dying as revealed in his John Brown essays and his late natural history essays, particularly "The Succession of Forest Trees." After assessing the transcendentalists' notions of heroism, it tracks Thoreau's early literary exposure to ideas of heroic dying, chastity, and virtue and considers his deep affinity for classical authors and his admiration of Native Americans.

Chapter 4 applies Thoreau's heightened sense of the mystical to the transition between living and dying. I principally focus on his two posthumously published books, *The Maine Woods* and *Cape Cod* as they connect to his thoughts about the transition between living and dying and the life of inanimate matter. I also touch on recent scholarship in the field of materiality studies, which offers a useful way to ponder Thoreau's relationship to objects.

Chapter 5 considers how Thoreau deliberately and naturally constructed his self-image and his legacy from his own dying. Even as he allowed his rough persona to soften under the ministrations of his family and friends, he refused all opiates and worked heroically to revise and prepare his works for posthumous publication. His dying gave him the chance to live in a kind of frozen present; he was suspended for many months in what must have felt like a timeless instant of transition. As I do throughout the book, I work in this chapter to understand just what Thoreau meant by his famous statement "one world at a time."[29]

II

What might a phrase such as "anticipation as prophecy" have meant to Thoreau, both in general and in relation to dying? He would have been familiar with *The Oxford English* dictionary's definition of the word as "the action of representing to oneself or realizing a thing before it occurs." Yet it is important to remember that *realizing,* as used in this definition, had a particular connotation in the nineteenth century. One could know something without realizing it. To realize it, one had to be able to create a picture of it in the mind, to imagine it, to understand it.[30] Likewise, Thoreau's contemporaries understood the word *prophecy* in particular ways. According to *The Oxford English Dictionary*'s first (now labeled obsolete) definition of the term, *prophecy* is "the action or practice of revealing or expressing the will or thought of God; divinely inspired utterance or discourse; the gift of this divine inspiration itself." This definition would have fit into the worldviews of most nineteenth-century Americans, who knew the Bible intimately. They were familiar, for instance, with the Old Testament story of the prophet Ezekiel, who tells the dry bones to reform themselves, grow sinews, and begin to breathe, even as that breath, in the form of a wind from God, is already sweeping through them.[31] Eighteen centuries later, the Romantics were still grasping the prophetic relation between the prophet-poet, the natural world, and the miraculous—commanding the winds to blow, the birds to call, and the waves to thunder.

Thoreau constantly incorporates this biblical sense into his anticipation of natural phenomena. For instance, in the "Housewarming" chapter in *Walden,* he describes the moment when he has finished his preparations for winter: "just as I had finished plastering, . . . the wind began to howl around the house as if it had not had permission to do so until then." Likewise, when, at the beginning of the book, he says, "To anticipate not the sunrise or the dawn merely but Nature herself!," he recalls biblical sources such these lines from Psalm 119: "I prevented the dawning of morning and cried: I hoped in thy word / Mine eyes prevent the night watches, that I might meditate in thy word."[32] Notably, both passages take a backward approach to time: the lines from the psalm begin with morning and end with the previous night; Thoreau puts the sunrise before the dawn. Though he did not read Hebrew, he was well versed in both the Bible and early modern poetry, and his writings picked up the nuances of the King James translation, which was the version available to nineteenth-century Americans.[33] Just as the biblical supplicant holds back the dawn to emphasize the circularity of his vigil, Thoreau anticipates the day's circularity by speeding past dawn to sunrise. The supplicant anticipates God's deliverance; Thoreau anticipates "Nature herself."[34]

Though the intention of God's deliverance in the Hebrew original meant a lengthening of temporal life, the Christian interpretation that Thoreau grew up with visualized a post-dying deliverance through God's son, associated rhetorically with the sun itself. Thus, Thoreau's sunrise is another deliverance. Faster than nature herself, he cycles through dawn, sunrise, and presumably forenoon, noon, afternoon, sunset, dusk, twilight, night, and then dawn again. The speed of human time as opposed to the eternity of natural time suggests a movement toward dying. Death itself may exist outside of nature, but the very idea of dying is nature hyper-stimulated. The supplicant in the psalm will gain his redemption, either by holding back death for a while longer or by embracing the gift it offers. By anticipating nature, the young surveyor by the pond will embrace it as the dying that turns the natural world.

This interpretation supports the famously obscure passage that precedes it: "I long ago lost a hound, a bay horse, and a turtledove, and am still on their trail."[35] What does Thoreau mean by "long ago"? As he has told us earlier in *Walden,* the Henry who lives at the pond is barely thirty years old. Thus, because "many travellers . . . seemed as anxious to discover [the animals] as if they had lost them themselves," most critics read his loss as a universal one and see the animals as symbols of loss. In this view, "long ago" is the indefinable eternity of natural time that humans can anticipate only by dying out of it. Conversely, however, one can read "long ago" as the vast record of human time and the fellow "travellers" as the many generations who have suffered the same temporal loss. While they may glimpse the animals or hear whispers of their sounds, those interactions are simply the anticipation of nature herself, a speeded-up circularity that places human temporality within the eternal present of natural time, a way of briefly holding back the dawn by pushing ahead of it and looking back.

Thoreau was also well versed in the old Puritan writings, to which he continually returned to learn about New England's Native Americans, the land and its animals, and the lives and livelihoods of the first English settlers.[36] Like most of his neighbors, he knew that the Puritans had avoided topping their steeples with a cross, preferring instead to use simple weathervanes. In Concord, the first steeple weathervane had been a simple five-sided brass arrow. More common was a rooster on a double perch that pointed out the four directions, which, according to tradition, served as a reminder and a warning of Peter's three denials of Christ the night before the crucifixion.[37] In my view, most Puritans would have seen a symbol of Peter's denial as a far greater offense than a cross on a steeple. I believe the weathervane cock meant no more to these earlier generations than the identical cocks on top of their barns: the very Thoreauvian, wake up early, be alert, labor at your vocation. But as time went by and people became more comfortable with religious symbolism, they were able to attach such imagery to objects.

The story of Peter was not only the explanation of the popularity of the weathervane cock; the rooster was also associated with ideas of resurrection, and its image was familiar in funerary customs. Between the early eighteenth and the early nineteenth centuries, for instance, many families of the deceased entertained their neighbors after funerals, often with small hard cakes served with ale or cider. These cakes, which might be prepared in the household, by the minister's or sexton's wife, or in a city bakeshop, were made in molds impressed with various designs, among them the crowing rooster. The historian William Woys Weaver has documented a bakeshop mold dating from 1785 that "depict[ed] an elaborately carved rooster, a symbol of resurrection and a popular motif on early American Funeral Biscuits."[38]

In *Walden*'s "Conclusion," Thoreau writes, "I don't suppose I have attained to obscurity," yet "in this part of the world it is considered a ground for complaint if a man's writings admit of more than one interpretation."[39] He himself, however, made use of multiple symbolic interpretations, as he demonstrates in a famous passage from "Life without Principle": "You come from attending the funeral of mankind to attend to a natural phenomenon. A little thought is sexton to all the world."[40] By "a little thought," does he mean a little thinking or a single original thought? According to his *Walden* remark, his neighbors would find either interpretation equally difficult. So why does he use "sexton" in his metaphor? A sexton is the person who digs graves and rings the church bell. Does "a little thought" wake humankind from its own funeral? Or does it complete the funeral with a burial? Could both readings be true? The remark recalls another of his beautiful paradoxes: "If a man does not keep pace with his companions perhaps it is because he hears a different drummer. It is not important he mature as soon as an apple-tree or an oak. Shall he turn his spring into summer?"[41] The answer is yes because a human's seasons are finite. We can never replicate a venerable tree's slow natural rhythm of living and dying over the course of countless rounds of seasons.

In *Walden*'s "Spring," Thoreau describes a pond that already reflects to his mortal eyes a summer sky, and he imagines the first robin song of summer. As a human being, he cannot help but turn his spring into summer;

this is both the gift and tragedy of his human consciousness. He writes, "The seasons went rolling on into summer, as one rambles into higher and higher grass," and then switches to an abrupt coda: "I finally left Walden September 6, 1847." He has turned his spring into fall.[42]

III

Thoreau's inspirations were not limited to the Christian teachings of his youth. Like many of the transcendentalists, he was also a devoted reader of eastern scripture. When he moved to Walden Pond on July 4, 1845, he carried with him only a handful of books. Among them were Homer's *Iliad* in the original Greek, which became the principle inspiration for *Walden's* third chapter, "Reading," and Charles Wilkins's 1785 translation of the Bhagavad Gita. Interestingly, both works feature a hero who does not want to fight. In the *Iliad,* anger prevents Achilles from acting, and an even greater anger compels him back into battle. In the Bhagavad Gita, Arjuna is sick at heart about the carnage that is about to ensue, but Krishna's arguments free him from complicity in death and ultimately in time. For very different reasons, each hero is reminded of his duty as a warrior and willingly turns back to the battle in which he is involved. Thoreau loved Krishna's argument about the unity of thought and action, even though he didn't find Krishna's ultimate argument—that it was Arjuna's duty to fight—particularly convincing. Yet as Robert Richardson writes, "from the Vedas, he drew a kind of Hindu stoicism," also noting a confluence between Thoreau's quest for liberation and Hindu teachings on the topic.[43]

For instance, liberation from time and from death are significant ideas in Thoreau's work. Similarly, in the Bhagavad Gita, Krishna assures Arjuna, "You speak sincerely but your sorrow has no cause. The wise grieve neither for the living nor the dead. There has never been a time when you and I and the kings gathered here did not exist, nor will there be a time when we cease to exist."[44] In the parable of the artist of Kouroo, which appears in *Walden's* "Conclusion," the artist's focus on his work removes him from the constraints of linear time. People and civilizations die around him, but he works on. At the end of his labor, his victory over time is complete:

> When the finishing stroke was put to his work, it suddenly expanded before the eyes of the astonished artist into the fairest of all the creations of Brahma . . . And now he saw by the heap of shavings at his feet, that

the former lapse of time had been an illusion, and that no more time had elapsed than is required of a single scintillation from the brain of Brahma to fall on and inflame the tinder of the mortal brain.[45]

In true transcendentalist fashion, the artist of Kouroo's thought becomes action; he finds liberation from time through spiritual discipline. According to the scholar Alan D. Hodder,

> Devotion, discipline and the pursuit of perfection are certainly some of the central values Thoreau's parable of Kouroo's artist intended to highlight, but the real key to the story is the impact of the artist's persevering devotion to his craft on the artist himself. Artistic creation . . . is not an end in itself but a discipline, a religious pursuit, whose value in the end accrues to the artist . . . The story of the artist of Kouroo represents an image of India molded according to the pressures of Thoreau's own religious and artistic vision. The Kouroo story is thus less biography than it is autobiography, in the Thoreauvian mode.[46]

Liberation from death also takes the disciple of Krishna outside of time. Krishna explains to Arjuna, "Those that remember me at the time of death will come to me . . . Whatever occupies the mind at the time of death determines the destination of the dying; always they will tend toward that state of being. Therefore, remember me at all times and fight on. When you make your mind one-pointed through regular meditation, you will find the supreme glory of the Lord."[47] This passage must have resonated with Thoreau, reflecting his own idea that we are always dying and must remain focused. If his friend William Ellery Channing can be trusted and Thoreau's last words were indeed "moose" and "Indian," then we know that he did remain focused to the end.[48] For him, "the supreme glory of the Lord" was life in nature, and at his moment of dying he was meditating on that life.

Krishna also says, "There are two paths, Arjuna, which the soul may follow at the time of death. One leads to rebirth and the other to liberation."[49] Rebirth in the eastern sense is reincarnation, or the transmigration of souls, in which the soul returns as either a less or a more spiritual being, depending on the creature's discipline during its previous life. Liberation is to go beyond rebirth, to that union with Krishna that ends the cycles of reincarnation. Thoreau, like Arjuna, yearned toward liberation yet was so fascinated by the steps involved in the cycles of rebirth that he translated from the French a section of the Harivamsa titled "The Transmigration of the Seven Brahmans." While earlier scholars have suggested Thoreau did this work while living at Walden, Richardson believes he translated it shortly after he left the Emerson home for good and returned to his own family, thus dating it between 1849 and 1850. This time frame makes sense to me: returning to his family would have reminded him of his lost brother, and the seven Brahmans are brothers.

In the tale, the brothers are disciples of the Brahman Gargya, and five of them yield to temptation and butcher Gargya's beautiful and beloved cow. Though they lie to their teacher, they do offer the murdered cow to the Pitris (the fathers). When the seven die, they come back as the seven sons of a hunter and his elderly wife. The sons devote themselves to holiness and, when their parents die, go to the woods to live contemplative lives. Because of their holiness, they next transmigrate into seven magnificent stags who devote themselves to contemplation and renunciation. So holy are their lives that they come back as geese and then as wild ducks performing acts of penitence. Three of the ducks are tempted by the splendor of Prince Vibhradja and must become men again. Ultimately, however, they are rewarded for their holy practices. Prince Vibhradja turns his throne over to his son and goes away to lead a holy life with the four ducks who did not stray. These four next come back as Brahmans, though the three who had strayed have no memory of their former existences. The four holy men remind the other three, the ones who strayed—a king and his two stewards—of their past lives, and the three immediately step down from their chariot and join the other four as Brahmans, thus becoming Brahmans themselves as well.

This tale would have been meaningful to Thoreau on a number of levels. The fact that some of the brothers betrayed their faith and discipline may have reminded him of the death of his own brother, who presumably moved into a higher realm while the recalcitrant brother was left behind. But I also think the consecutive animal reincarnations would have resonated with him. It may seem logical to the western mind that the first animal transmigration changed them from the sons of a hunter to mighty and magnificent stags. But as the brothers reach into higher and holier existence, they become smaller animals. After being ducks they finally transmigrate into Brahmans. This bird imagery spoke to Thoreau who saw birds, both in themselves and as metaphor, as "winged thoughts."[50] In a parable in *Walden,* he takes the transmigration pattern to an even smaller level, describing the "beautiful bug" that frees itself from an old applewood table:

> Who does not feel his faith in a resurrection and immortality strength-ened by hearing this? Who knows what beautiful winged life, whose eggs have been buried for ages under many concentric circles of woodenness in the dead dry life of society, deposited at first in the aburnum of the green and living tree, which has gradually been converted into the sem-blance of its own well-seasoned tomb,—heard perchance gnawing out now for years by the astonished family of man, as they sat around the festive board,—may unexpectedly come forth from amidst society's most trivial and handselled furniture, to enjoy its perfect summer at last![51]

Just as the artist of Kouroo reflects the Bhagavad Gita's liberation from time in the transformation of the artist through his work, the beautiful bug represents the Hindu understanding (though Thoreau does use the very Christian word "resurrection") of liberation from death. Thoreau is the artist and the beautiful bug. As autobiography, the parable gives the reader a portrait of the man at Walden, a soul striving toward liberation, who, through contemplation and discipline, is free from a numbing death in antebellum society to lead at last a true and extravagant life.

IV

In *Walden*'s "Conclusion," Thoreau writes, "I learned this, at least, by my experiment; that if one advances confidently in the direction of his dreams, and endeavors to live the life he imagined, he will meet with a success unexpected in common hours."[52] At first glance this statement appears to be a joyous and triumphant one, triggered primarily by the word "success." Yet the sentence is also filled with heartbreak. The man who had planned to "brag as lustily as chanticleer" concludes his book by saying that he has learned "at least" something from his "experiment," which suggests that there was far more that he did not learn. Moreover, he explicitly does not say our dreams will come true. Rather, the success that we do achieve will not often be recognizable "in common hours." Only in isolated moments of thought and inspiration will we be able to see that we have gained some-thing precious.

In the chapter titled "The Bean-Field," Thoreau considers moral and spiritual failure, which he frames as experience:

This further experience I also gained. I said to myself, I will not plant beans and corn with so much industry another summer, but such seed, if the seed is not lost, as sincerity, truth, simplicity, innocence, and the like, and see if they will not grow in this soil . . . and sustain me, for surely it has not been exhausted for these crops. Alas! I said this to myself; but now another summer is gone, and another, and another, and I am obliged to say to you, Reader, that the seeds which I planted, if indeed they *were* the seeds of those virtues, were wormeaten, or had lost their vitality, and so did not come up.[53]

Earlier in the book, Thoreau describes planting a smaller crop during his second summer at the pond so as to have more time for other pursuits, and we know he lived at Walden for only two summers. Thus, the quoted passage is not about husbandry but about the embryo virtues—"Sincerity, truth, simplicity, and innocence"—he hoped to cultivate. But his seeds have not germinated, and he must face up to both the death of dreams and the death of virtues.

Dying was on Thoreau's mind when he went to the pond in 1845 to write a first draft of *A Week on the Concord and Merrimack Rivers.* Yet even though it was an elegy to his dead brother, the sense of renewal he reveals in this book is strong. *Walden,* however, is a story of the process of dying. Thoreau begins his story in March, describing ice breakup, snowmelt, and songbird migration. As the year cycles past, however, the subsequent winter becomes an avatar of himself and, in that sense, the hero of the book. Thus, the second spring he describes, celebrated in all its beauty and promise, is also shown as the slow, brave dying of winter: "One attraction of coming to the woods to live was that I should have leisure and opportunity to see the spring come in."[54] He is a spectator of spring but also isolated from it.

Birds and bird imagery are important signifiers of his state of mind. Early in *Walden,* Thoreau writes, "On the first of April it rained and melted the ice, and in the early part of the day, which was very foggy, I heard a stray goose groping about over the pond and cackling as if lost, or like the spirit of the fog." In the subsequent chapter, he then makes one of his startlingly paradoxical statements. He begins by describing his house, which had "a clean and airy look, especially in the morning, when its timbers were saturated with dew . . . To my imagination it retained throughout the day more or less of this auroral character." Then, few sentences later, he writes, "The Harivansa [*sic*] says, 'An abode without birds is like meat without seasoning.' Such was not my abode, for I found myself suddenly neighbor to the birds; not by having imprisoned one, but having caged myself near them."[55] The use of "cage" as a description for a house that clearly delights him is startling, as is the Harivamsa quotation associating "birds" and "meat."

In the chapter "Spring," he continues to create these surprising connections:

> Suddenly, an influx of light filled my house, though the evening was at hand, and the clouds of winter overhung it . . . I looked out the window, and lo! Where yesterday was cold, gray ice there lay the transparent pond already calm and full of hope as on a summer evening, reflecting a summer evening in its bosom, though none was visible overhead . . . As it grew darker, I was startled by the *honking* of geese flying low over the woods, like weary travellers . . . indulging at last in unrestrained complaint and mutual consolation. Standing at my door I could hear the rush of their wings; when driving toward my house, they suddenly spied my light, and with hushed clamor wheeled and settled on the pond. So I came in and shut the door, and passed my first spring night in the woods.[56]

Paradoxically, by going inside and closing the door to avoid frightening the geese, he does not pass his first spring night in the woods but spends it caged away from nature. The geese's "mutual consolation" emphasizes his solitude. Though he has mentioned many times how much he loves to be alone, he nonetheless seems to suffer isolation for want of the right society, which is exactly what the geese have. This notion is reinforced later in the chapter, when a lost goose again makes an appearance, this time aurally rather than visually: "For a week I heard the circling groping clangor of some solitary goose in the foggy mornings, seeking its companion, and still peopling the woods with a larger life than they could sustain."[57] Like Thoreau, the goose suffers solitude because his expectations of society exceed what is available.

Other birds also have important roles in *Walden*—for instance, the merlin hawk, which "appeared to have no companion in the universe,— sporting there alone, and to need none but the morning and the ether with which it played. It was not lonely, but made all the earth lonely beneath it."[58] Thoreau often but not always sees the merlin as the triumph of his solitary self. In the chapter "Brute Neighbors," Thoreau also introduces a diving loon. In an apparent battle with his divided self, he keeps trying to guess where the bird will next surface on the pond. The loon always wins but then, Thoreau-like, gives himself away with his laughter, "calling on the god of loons" for rain.[59] In the end, though, the loon is destined to lose a different game, as Thoreau demonstrates in his description of the dead loons shot by hunters.

Thoreau prepared the second edition of *Walden* in early 1862, while he was dying. At that time he changed the title from *Walden, or a Life in the Woods* to simply *Walden*. In "Spring" he had written of leaving the pond because he had "many other lives to live," even though much of his subsequent work continued to stay close to those environs. Perhaps the "life" of his Walden experiment was one more way of living in the world that his experiences had created. It was a dying life in the most natural sense because no one individual life—human, plant, or animal—endures very long in natural time. By changing to a spatial title rather than a temporal one, Thoreau allowed his one life at the pond, like the vanishing dent of his cellar hole, to step into the universal cycle.

1

Figure in the Mist
The Death of John Thoreau, Jr.

Verily the Thoreaus as a family knew how to die as bravely as
they lived.

—ANNIE RUSSELL MARBLE, *Thoreau:*
His Friends, Home, and Books

I

Thoreau honed his lifelong talent for remembering both dead persons
and dead times in the pages of his first book, *A Week on the Concord and
Merrimack Rivers,* an elegy to his older brother, John Thoreau, Jr.[1] Thoreau
had an early and ongoing relationship to dying: the Emerson and Thoreau
families both suffered from poor health, and Thoreau had continually confronted loss and early death. Most painful was the death of his brother, to
whom he had been tremendously close. Yet despite that closeness, Thoreau
had moved away from his family in his early twenties and aligned himself
with Ralph Waldo Emerson, living first in Emerson's home in Concord,
then in his brother William's home on Staten Island, then on Emerson's
woodlot on Walden Pond, and then again in the Emerson house in Concord. Yet Thoreau may have felt some guilt in leaving his own family, especially given that John was stricken with his final illness while he was gone.

In *A Week on the Concord and Merrimack Rivers,* we see the young writer
growing into his solitary adulthood as he takes stock of his personal losses
and the losses of time and history. The death of his beloved brother becomes
a metaphor for all loss, and nature becomes both the repository of loss
and the only fact Thoreau can turn to for both its realization and release.

The book combines the recollection of a long-ago pleasure excursion with the present moment of writing to form a monument not in stone, which Thoreau would have rejected, but in words. Until Thoreau's own death twenty years later, John remained to his brother a figure from the mystical, immutable, and innocent past. Yet unlike Emerson, who went so far as to open the coffins of his first wife and his eldest son, Thoreau never mentioned the grave of his brother, not even in letters or his Journal.

January 1842 was a horrible month for the Emerson and Thoreau families. On New Year's Day, John cut his finger while stropping his razor. The cut was a trifling one, and he wrapped his finger in a cloth and did not worry about it. In a little more than a week, he discovered that the cut had "mortified," and on the next day he was stricken with lockjaw, or tetanus.[2] The doctors could do nothing to prevent his agonizing death. Yet according to Thoreau's biographer, Robert Richardson, "John accepted the fact that he was going to die calmly and with fortitude that was both Stoic and Christian: 'The cup that my father gives me, shall I not drink it?'" John died a day and a half later in Henry's arms. He was twenty-six years old.[3]

Thoreau was devastated but held his feelings in check: family members noted that he barely spoke, took no interest in the outdoors, and seemed to register no emotion. Then, to their horror, he, too, began to develop lockjaw symptoms, although he had no wound. For a time, his family and friends believed they were about to lose him as well, but in a January 24 letter Emerson reported, "This morning his affection, be what it may, is relieved, & essentially, & what is best, his own feeling of better health is established."[4] Nonetheless, Thoreau remained lethargic for many months. In the weeks following John's death, he went outside only with the aid of his sisters, and he wrote nothing in his Journal for more than two months. According to Richardson, "even his interest in nature was gone; he was 'denaturalized,' as he later admitted to a correspondent."[5]

But the month's tragedies were not over. Just as Thoreau was recovering, the Emersons' precocious and cherished five-year-old son, Ralph Waldo, Jr., came down with scarlet fever and died three days later.[6] There had long been an attachment between John Thoreau and little Waldo. During the previous summer, for instance, a traveling daguerreotypist had come to Concord. Both Henry (who, like his brother, was good with children) and Emerson's wife, Lidian, had tried to get Waldo to sit for a likeness, but the boy was too restless to sit still for the long exposure required. On the next day, however, John took Waldo back to the daguerreotypist and managed to keep him still for the entire five-minute exposure. This precious daguerreotype was the only image the Emersons ever had of their lost child. Many years later, in 1865, Emerson would write in his journal, "John Thoreau, Junior, knew how much I would value a head of little Waldo, then five years old . . . He did it, & brought me the daguerre which I thankfully paid for. In a few months, after my boy died, and I have ever since, had deeply to thank John Thoreau for that wise & gentle piece of friendship."[7]

Both John and Waldo died suddenly of illnesses that would be curable today. But the Emersons and the Thoreaus were also haunted by another disease—consumption, or tuberculosis, which for several centuries was known as "the New England Disease."[8] In 1867, Oliver Wendell Holmes, Sr., told his incoming Harvard medical students, "'Every other resident adult you meet . . . in these streets is or will be more or less tuberculous. This is not an extravagant estimate as nearly one third of the deaths of adults in Boston last year were from phthisis.'"[9]

When Emerson was eleven, he lost his father to consumption. When he was a young man, his two brilliant younger brothers succumbed, as did his adored first wife, Ellen, who died just before her twentieth birthday, after they had been married for only eighteen months. Emerson suffered from the disease for his entire life but managed, by dint of rest and will-power, to keep it under control. He would die of pneumonia at the age of seventy-nine. The Thoreau family was even harder hit by consumption. The first recorded victim was John Thoreau, Henry's grandfather, who died of the disease in 1801 at the age of forty-seven.[10] Henry's older sister Helen succumbed in 1849, his father in 1859. According to friends and family, his mother lived with the disease until she was eighty-five, when she finally died of it. John, Jr., was suffering acutely from consumption at the time of his death. No longer able to work at the school he and Henry had founded, he was frighteningly thin and coughing blood. Most likely he developed tetanus from a minor cut because the tuberculosis had destroyed his immune system.

Henry Thoreau himself died from consumption in 1862 when he was only forty-four years old. Though he struggled with the disease all his life, he never referred to it by name, preferring to say he had a bad cold, the ague, or bronchitis. His first recorded bout occurred in 1836, when he was a nineteen-year-old Harvard student, and he had to come home for a semester. In 1843, Emerson wrote in his journal about how pleased he was that Thoreau was on the mend from his most recent bout of bronchitis.[11] After the publication of *Walden* in 1854, Thoreau suffered a debilitating weakness in his legs, most likely linked to consumption, which lasted for more than a year. For most of his life, he suffered from a constant cough that worsened every winter. Emerson's son, Edward Waldo, who grew up to become a doctor, later suggested that Thoreau's illness may have been exacerbated by the fine dust he breathed in while helping to run the family's pencil and graphite business.[12]

Treatment of consumption was primitive. The most benign approach was the recommendation that patients spend time in a warm climate. In the 1820s, Emerson took that advice and visited Saint Augustine, Florida, for several months to strengthen his lungs. Doctors also used blisters (which involved applying plaster mixed with ground cantharides and stimulants such as pepper and mustard to the skin until a blister rose), bled patients, and suggested that a "jolting" horse or carriage ride could "loosen" the disease from the lungs.[13] Two days before her February death, Ellen Emerson dutifully rode out on horseback and in a buggy in a desperate attempt to regain her health. Thoreau, however, wisely refused all of his doctors' remedies. Though he did travel to warm, dry Minnesota less than a year before his death, he was probably more interested in the region's plants than in the salubriousness of the climate.

II

At the time of his brother's fatal illness, Henry had been living with the Emerson family for several months. After moving back home temporarily after John's death, he returned to them and, as I have mentioned, spent a number of years in various Emerson households. His rationale at the time was his need, as a writer, for quiet. The Thoreaus, especially his mother, were talkative; in addition, she took in boarders to help support the family financially. At the Emersons, he received room and board in exchange for doing some gardening and carpentry, and he had ample quiet for study and writing. Lidian and the children adored him and were dependent on him in many ways, particularly when Emerson was lecturing away from home. But the most compelling feature of the Emerson home was the vast library to which Thoreau had free access.

Some biographers have described the Thoreaus as impoverished yokels. In truth, however, they were a reading family, and all four of the children taught school. Mrs. Thoreau stinted on household luxuries such as meat and tea in order to purchase a piano for her two daughters, a way to not only increase their value as teachers but also to put the family squarely within the decorous middle class. Likewise, the whole family, aunts included, worked and saved to pay for Henry's Harvard expenses. At least three of the children could read and write Latin fluently, and Henry and Helen sometimes corresponded in that language. Nonetheless, they were not a family of intellectuals. Unlike the transcendentalists, they enjoyed popular fiction; and until 1850, when Thoreau set up his attic study and library at the Yellow House, none of their houses had a room set apart for study, reading, and philosophical discussion. Thoreau was one of the first family members to attend college, whereas Emerson was descended from seven generations of ministers. The intellectuals and cranks of the day gathered at the Emerson home to discuss "the newness," Plato, reason, and understanding.[14] In contrast, the Thoreaus enjoyed gossiping with their neighbors.

John and Henry Thoreau had always been close. John was the first to begin studying botany in the fields and woods and later taught his younger brother what he knew. John and his father were both excellent flutists, and Henry presumably learned to play from them; the whole family sang. Concord was a small town, and no doubt John and Henry continued to see each often, even after Thoreau aligned himself with the Emersons. But even though generations of critics have blamed Henry's somatic lockjaw on guilt about courting the same girl, I suspect that much of his distress stemmed from his separation from his brother.

Like many Romantics, Thoreau worshipped the notion of childhood. Even as a very young man, he felt a terrible sense of loss at leaving that period of his life. His Journal is full of descriptions of young boys that are imbued with vicarious pleasure and deep sorrow, and John was a unique link to his own boyhood. In 1837, when he returned home after graduating from Harvard, Thoreau wrote to both Helen and John, who were away teaching. The letter to Helen is affectionate and playful, typical of an adult sibling; the writer explains that brevity does not indicate a lack of fondness, tells her that not much of interest is going on, and avoids burdening her with trivialities. The letter to John is very different. In it, he "plays Indian," as the two must have done as boys. He calls himself "Tahatawan" the sachem and refers to his "brother sachem" as Hopewell. He labels the local politicians as "the pale faces," also calling them "squaws" to signify their powerlessness: "There is no seat for Tahatawan in the council-house. He lets the squaws speak." He cleverly uses conventionalized Native American dialect to satirize local politics and a lyceum lecture, and one gets the impression that this had been a familiar boyhood way of communicating with one another.[15]

In the fall of 1838, Henry and John opened a school for boys and girls. At first the school met in the family home; but as enrollment expanded, the brothers took over the vacant Concord Academy, and out-of-town children boarded at the Thoreau home. There they joined the adult boarders already in residence. Among Mrs. Thoreau's favorites were Mrs. Joseph Ward and her unmarried middle-aged daughter Prudence Ward. When their eleven-year-old grandson and nephew, Edmund Sewall, came to visit in June 1839, Henry was immediately taken with him. Soon after the boy left, Henry addressed a poem to him, titled "Sympathy."[16]

Critics have long argued about this poem, and not only about whether it does or does not have homoerotic overtones. Many also wonder if references to the "gentle boy" conceal the true topic of the poem, the boy's seventeen-year-old sister, Ellen Sewall, with whom both Thoreau brothers would later fall in love.[17] Yet strangely all of these arguments disregard the poem's title. In the nineteenth century, *sympathy* did not connote a polite form of pity but meant fellow feeling. Two people in sympathy understood one another. Moreover, critics overlook the fact that the poem is an elegy. But for whom? Edmund was a healthy boy, and he was enrolled in the Thoreau brothers' school during the following term. Ellen was also strong and healthy. After two visits to Concord, she went on to marry a Unitarian minister and live a long life.

In my view, Thoreau is writing about his lost boyhood, which he sees reflected in the "gentle boy." "Sympathy" opens with the following stanza:

> Lately alas, I knew a gentle boy,
> Whose features all were cast in Virtue's mold,
> As one she had designed for Beauty's toy,
> But after manned him for her own stronghold.

"Virtue," in the classical sense, implies an innocence associated with forbearance, continence, and bravery—a perfect boyhood—and several stanzas later we encounter the sense of personal loss Thoreau feels in the contemplation of this state:

> We two were one while we did sympathize
> So could we not the simplest bargain drive;
> And what avails it now that we are wise,
> If absence does this doubleness contrive?

In other words, as long as the man and the boy see nature by the same lights, they can function as one entity. But the knowledge that comes from the man's fallen nature separates him from the boy's natural wisdom and creates this terrible absence and loss.

The poem ends with a last attempt to create sympathy between the boy and the man through the aegis of nature, which is never fallen:

> If I but love that virtue which he is,
> Though it be scented in the morning air,
> Still shall we be truest acquaintances,
> Nor mortals know a sympathy more rare.[18]

The poem mourns the loss of the sympathy Thoreau could have had with Edmund Sewall if he still possessed the innocence of nature that among humans is only the provenance of children.

In early September 1839, not long after the brothers had returned home after their two-week excursion on the Concord and Merrimack rivers, John set off for Ellen's home in Scituate to propose. She said yes but reneged after consulting her father. Then on November 4, 1840, Henry mailed Ellen his own proposal. This time Ellen consulted her father first and sent Henry a brief refusal. The Thoreau brothers' double courtship of Ellen Sewall is echoed in the doubling of their consciousness in *A Week on the Concord and Merrimack Rivers,* where we repeatedly see Henry's tendency to participate in the social world via his brother's experience and then to engage in the same experience himself: "Occasionally one [brother] ran along the shore . . . visiting the nearest farm-houses, while the other followed the windings of the stream alone to meet his companion at some distant point, and hear the report of his adventures."[19] In the memory of the surviving brother, Ellen's double rejection completed the doubleness of the courtship: the loss of the girl and the loss of his brother became one fact in the act of remembering.

It can be difficult to integrate this ardent young man with the deliberately aloof and asexual mature Thoreau. Ellen Sewall was an extremely pretty girl—lively, intelligent, and enthusiastic. Apparently the Thoreau brothers weren't the only young men in Concord who tried to woo her, though she seems to have favored the stern and awkward Henry. Richardson writes, "Her first thank-you letter [to her aunt], written immediately after her first trip to Concord, is surprising by its excess . . . The event was barely over, but already it is treated as a distant and treasured past. Over a year later, after John's proposal but before Henry's, she wrote again to her aunt about Concord in the same elegiac fashion, as though reconciled to losses eons ago."[20] Perhaps a shared attraction to memorializing the past at the instant of its transition from the present drew the young Thoreau to her. For instance, in the chapter titled "Sunday," he writes, "On this same stream a maiden once sailed in my boat, thus unattended except by invisible guardians, and as she sat in the prow there was nothing but herself between the steersman and the sky." In the real time of the narrative, both brothers had rowed the same maiden on the same river just weeks before. But by changing the first person to "the steersman" Thoreau not only calls up the brothers' tandem courtship but also makes the experience archetypal. "Such is the never-failing beauty and accuracy of language, the most perfect art in the world; the chisel of a thousand years retouches it."[21] In 1839, the rivalry over Ellen must have been a pressingly present reality between the brothers. But with John's death in 1842, the whole meaning of the dual courtship must have changed. Ellen, like her brother Edmund, became a figure of memory, subject to the chisel.

Many of Thoreau's poems from the late 1830s appear in *A Week,* but the inclusion of "Sympathy" is particularly interesting. As the epitome of all "lovely boys," John Thoreau seems to stand in for Edmund as the lost boy who can be accessed only through nature. Thus, the poem and the book as a whole become, like the maiden on the river, both an elegy and an archetype.

III

In the chapter "Thursday," Thoreau briefly explains that he and John stow their boat and hike for six days. In other words, they leave the river on Thursday morning and return on the following Thursday evening and so spend their single week completing a circuit of the rivers. This circularity is not only fundamental to Thoreau's view of experience but also enhances the reader's anticipation of the cycle, which in turn informs the theme and structure of the book. Each chapter mimics that overall structure: during digressions, we anticipate a return to the temporal narrative; during the narrative, we anticipate the various disquisitions on poetry, history, philosophy, and friendship.

Thoreau begins his story in the first-person singular and contemplates the river in the past perfect—"I had often stood on the banks of the Concord"—thereby indicating a layered past. He remembers remembering that past: "The chips and weeds and occasional logs and stems of trees that floated past, fulfilling their fate, were objects of singular interest to me."[22] Here, *singular* carries more than one definition. In addition to meaning "particular," it emphasizes the speaker's solitude, the absolute "I" of his remembrance. After long contemplation, he, like the detritus on the river, will allow himself to drift with the current—in this case, into the narrative of how "we" evolved into "I."

Heroic dying is a significant element of *A Week,* one underscored by Thoreau's frequent references to ancient poetry. Over the course of the narrative, this allows him to project his brother into a natural-heroic dialectic. The book, like nature, will speak in a timeless language that keeps his brother alive in his youth, at a moment of perfect physical and psychic ripeness, just before his fall into death. Thoreau writes, "For their beauty, consider the fables of Narcissus, of Endymion, of Memnon son of morning, the representative of all promising youths who have died a premature death, and whose memory is prolonged to the latest morning."[23] Morning, he will later say in *Walden,* always brings back the heroic age, and beautiful youths who die young will always live in that age.

Anticipation plays a principal role in Thoreau's use of time, which switches from the present moment of his writing, back to excursions after his brother's death, back to the late summer of 1839 when the two journeyed up the rivers together. For example, in "Sunday," he discusses how the railroads have since changed the landscape of 1839: "But the real vessels are the railroad cars, and its main stream . . . may be traced by a long line of vapor amid the hills which no morning wind ever disperses."[24] By making the present past, he predicts an altered world his brother will never know.

In an Emersonian moment earlier in the chapter, Thoreau writes,

"Mythology is only the most ancient history and biography. So far from being false or fabulous in the common sense, it contains only enduring and essential truth, the I and you, the here and there, the now and then, being omitted. Either time or rare wisdom writes it."[25] Throughout *A Week*, he consciously creates a mythology of a time that seems as long ago as the Indian wars are yet is deeply felt in the present. As he does in "Ktaadn," he plays with the idea of common sense as a shared sensation that touches all people regardless of time, place, or identity.[26] Time steps back from time-lessness and bears it witness.

In "Monday," Thoreau notes that, "our reflections anticipated our prog-ress somewhat,—we were advancing farther into the country and into the day." In this pun he once again conflates the spatial and the temporal as the brothers adumbrate themselves into new epochs and vistas. Just as their shadows and thoughts anticipate their progress, Thoreau's prophecy of his brother's shadow presages the narrative: "You must be calm before you can utter oracles . . . Enthusiasm is a supernatural serenity."[27] His description of the brothers' youthful enthusiasm anticipates the serenity of his descrip-tion of the river and, in a larger sense, the serenity he needed to record and mythologize his singular narrative (that is, the retreat to Walden Pond).

In the following sentence, Thoreau creates a particularly arresting image of his brother: "The crowd stood admiring the mist and the dim outlines of the trees seen through it, when one of their number advanced to explore the phenomenon, and with fresh admiration all eyes were turned on his dimly retreating figure." The description echoes the poem that appears in his book's head note, in which he calls on his brother to be his muse.[28] The fact that the viewers are studying a natural phenomenon emphasizes the physicality of nature even in the midst of philosophical musing; yet even without physicality, John remains a figure in the landscape. Similarly, a few pages later, Thoreau points out that "there where it seemed uninterrupted forest to our youthful eyes, between two neighboring pines in the horizon, lay the valley of the Nashua."[29] Once again, he looks through the mist into something glorious—an entire pine forest seen through the frame of the emblematic double pine trees. In his vision, the young brothers antic-ipate a rarefied, always youthful, version of themselves with all the world before them—images that both challenge and conflate the fleeting and the permanent.

Just as the tandem existence of the brothers is reflected in the two pine trees, their tandem activity is mirrored in the wild pigeons and the pair of red squirrels that Thoreau writes about in "Tuesday." Although the birds had filled the sky in the morning, they "now like ourselves [are] spending their noon in the shade." A few sentences later he offers a more ominous meaning for shade, telling us that he and John took advantage of the pigeons' rest by killing one of them. Mocking his own ideas of dying and heroism, Thoreau notes that he and John persevered "heroically" by gutting and spitting the bird that he feels should have been left alive. He then expands the idea into a questioning of dying and nature: "Nature herself has not provided the most graceful end for her creatures . . . We do not see the bodies lie about . . . They must perish miserably; not one of them is translated."[30]

Earlier in the scene Thoreau has described the antics of two red squirrels, who run together among the pine trees, warning each other of the brothers' approach, "devising through what safe valve of frisk or somerset to let [their] . . . superfluous life escape."[31] We do not learn until many pages later that the brothers have killed their squirrel counterparts. They discover, however, that they cannot eat them, as they did the pigeon; instead, they throw away their skinned little bodies and eat rice. Likening the squirrels to larger animals, Thoreau lets the reader take the intuitive leap from cattle to men. Despite their refusal to eat the squirrels, the brothers have added to the invisible carnage of nature. Moreover, while the killing of one pigeon suggests John's death, the murder of the two squirrels contains the larger implication of the death of both brothers.

At the end of "Sunday," Thoreau draws a contrast between himself and his brother: "One sailor was visited in his dreams by the Evil Destinies this night . . . which constrain and oppress the minds of men. But the other happily passed a serene and even ambrosial or immortal night, . . . a happy natural sleep until the morning; and his cheerful spirit soothed and reassured his brother, for wherever they meet, the Good Genius is sure to prevail."[32] With the exception of the head note, this is the only passage in the book that implicitly describes the dead brother as an ever-present guiding spirit; and once again Thoreau uses grammar to conflate his narratives. "This night" puts the moment in the present, and "whenever they meet" implies a relationship that will not end. Thus, the many other journeys that he describes in the narrative are continuations of this central journey.

One of those resonating journeys is a hike up Saddleback Mountain.

At dusk, when Thoreau reaches the summit, he notes the remnants that other campers have left and rhapsodizes humorously about the newspapers in which they had wrapped their food. As always, however, humor signals a serious intention, and the advertisements in the newspapers come to signify the last vestiges of the civilized world. Thoreau tells us that he has arrived at the summit without water or blankets. While his lack of preparation may seem strange, given his long experience as an outdoorsman, we may read this scene as essentially a psychic excursion into dying. He describes creating a coffin-like shelter for himself: "I at length completely encased myself in boards, managing even to put a board on top of me with a large stone to hold it down."[33] When he rises from his improvised coffin in the morning, he finds himself in a different world, one reminiscent of the "ambrosial, immortal" dream landscape of his brother's happy sleep. Thoreau recalls, "As the light increased I discovered around me an ocean of mist, which . . . shut out every vestige of the earth, while I was left floating on this fragment of the wreck of the world, on my carved plank in cloud-land. . . . the new *terra firma* perchance of my future life." He imagines himself in "the dazzling halls of Aurora," the home of heroic youths who die young. "It was such a country as we might see in dreams, with all the delights of paradise." But he is still part of the temporal world so cannot remain in the dream landscape. The mist eventually dissipates, and he must climb down into "the region of cloud and drizzling rain, . . . [where] the inhabitants affirmed it had been a cloudy and drizzly day wholly."[34]

Throughout "Tuesday," Thoreau continues to conflate and challenge the fleeting and the permanent, prophesying that "when out of history the truth shall be extracted, it will have shed its dates like withered leaves."[35] He adds to his discussion of prophetic timelessness in "Wednesday," when he considers the inanimate life of rock. Stones are pulled into "new freshets receiving the aid of fresh stones, which are drawn into this trap . . . until they either wear out, or wear through the bottom of their prison, or else are released by some revolution of Nature . . . In one instance . . . [the freshets] have worn quite through the rock, so that a portion of the river leaks through in anticipation of the fall."[36] Water and rock exist in slow time, in patterns and cycles that are hard to comprehend. Thoreau's conflation of the fleeting and the permanent reminds us that permanence is a human construct: everything on the river has lived a past. He writes, "The finest workers in stone are not copper or steel tools, but the gentle touches of air and water working at their leisure with an ample allowance of time" and notes that the Hindu and Chinese philosophers, who "reach back to the time when the race of mortals is confounded with the race of gods, are as nothing compared with the periods which these stones have inscribed."[37] The loss of John is a trickle of water on these ancient rocks.

As the previous passage demonstrates, Thoreau's writing in *A Week* was influenced not only by the eastern texts he was reading and translating, but also by the work of Charles Lyell and other geologists, who were now beginning to decipher the age of the earth. Thoreau was a close follower of his era's scientific progress; and as the historian Laura Dassow Walls explains, "one of the fascinations of nineteenth-century science was the way geology had learned to loop together time and space, such that natural objects assemble as temporal layers."[38] Thus, the writer's meditation on rocks and water becomes the perfect introduction to his meditation on friendship. Like the rocks, the friend he describes is covered with the "dust of Nature." True friendship is "a drama that is always tragic" because it is aligned with nature's "incessant tragedies"—that is, always in the process of dying. "When they say farewell then we begin to keep them company."[39]

By re-creating his journey with his brother, Thoreau writes from the vantage point of pure friendship—a shared consciousness. Telling us that most friends "are not transfigured and translated by love in each other's presence," he entertains the idea that translation *is* possible in true friendships, such as the one that exists with John: "They are few and rare, indeed, but like a strain of music, they are incessantly repeated and modulated by the memory."[40] In a sense, Thoreau can hear strains of John through memory—music that is always varied and fresh, much like the young streams feeding the river on which they row. As friendship exists in memory, so does it exist in anticipation: "It requires immaculate and godlike qualities full-grown, and exists only by condescension and anticipation."[41] Thus, Thoreau emphasizes friendship's prophetic timelessness, as he will later also do in *Walden*. By dying, John will always exist to inspire his brother to emulation.

In "Friday," Thoreau writes, "In human intercourse the tragedy begins, not where there is misunderstanding about words, but when silence is misunderstood."[42] Here again he introduces tragedy into friendship. Because silence encompasses all knowledge, to misunderstand a friend's silence is to be blind and deaf to him. John's dying created a profound silence in his

brother's life, but to misunderstand this silence would be to deny that John
ever existed. Within this profound silence, there can be no mere exchange
of words, no explanation. Only in memory and anticipation can his consciousness be shared without misunderstanding. Whereas memory brings
the living friend to that dying moment, anticipation intimates that he and
his friend will soon share a profound silence in an ethereal world. Anticipation and memory form a circle, just as "the latest November" is the same
as "the ruddy morning of youth."[43] Boundaries dissolve; to love the friend
is to love nature. In this sense, there is a synthesis of consciousness (the
Emerson me) and nature (the not me). "Even the death of Friends will
inspire us as much as their lives."[44]

Dying is the final expression of the sublimity of friendship. Rather
than being trapped in the time and place of the graveyard, the dead
friend moves through them in the eternal present, "the meeting of two
eternities."[45] At the end of the chapter, Thoreau writes, "I dreamed this
night . . . of a difference with a Friend . . . But in the dream ideal justice
was at length done me for his suspicions and I received that compensation
which I had never obtained in my waking hours."[46] Dreams are generated by that ethereal world in which his friend lives and where Thoreau
believes he will one day also live. In this ideal realm all misunderstandings
are silenced and all hurts are compensated. In dying, the friend is more
strongly present than ever.

In "Thursday," Thoreau depicts the brothers as they "lie drenched on a
bed of withered wild oats" when they wake in the morning.[47] In this pregnant image, the wild oats, a symbol of youthful adventuring, wither away
even as they are sensuously drenched and seemingly full of life. Thoreau
follows this image with an untitled poem in which he casts off his books so
as to be fully engaged in nature, living "a purely sensuous life."[48] The point
of view is first-person singular, and the poet is alone in nature, recount-
ing the past and bringing it up to the present time of the poem. Thoreau
moves on to observe ants, dew, and clouds, and says, "I am well drenched
upon my bed of oats."[49] In this way, he embeds himself in consecutive historical presents that are in fact two layers of the past. Doubly, then singly,
the young men and the young man have lain on the wet withering oats,
and then they have passed on. Paradoxically, the poet shrugs off the call of
books in order to be in nature, but the moment cannot continue to exist

except in the leaves of a book. The brothers on their bed of oats remain more distant and more obscure without this book of remembrance.

Later in the chapter, Thoreau writes, "In the wildest nature, there is not only the material of the most cultivated life, and a sort of anticipation of the last result, but a greater refinement already than is ever attained by any man."[50] "Last result" implies, if not the end of time, then the end of a completed cycle. This result is anticipated in nature by a "greater refinement" than man outside of nature can achieve—another Thoreauvian paradox that conflates time. His notion is that future humans, through self-cultivation, will become less coarse and more refined, yet in nature that moment of fruition exists fully in the present. Thus, the present moment is "later" than the passage in which he lay alone on his bed of wild oats, and this fruitfulness anticipates the continued presence of the lost brother in the present.

In his subsequent writings, Thoreau often returned to the trope of western orientation. As he knew, Celtic tradition suggests that to turn west is to turn toward dying; and when he borrowed this meaning in his work, he was both punning on and mocking the burgeoning notion of manifest destiny. In both *A Week* and *Walden,* the end of the day is an important moment. As he writes in "Thursday,"

> In deep ravines under the eastern sides of cliffs, Night forwardly plants her foot even at noonday, and even as the day retreats she steps into his trenches, skulking from tree to tree . . . It may be said that the forenoon is brighter than the afternoon . . . because we naturally look into the west, as forward into the day, and so in the forenoon see the sunny side of things, but in the afternoon the shadow of every tree.[51]

To look forward into the day is to anticipate its end; and just as each day of the week's journey comes to an end, so must the journey itself end. In keeping with this pattern, Thoreau constructed "Thursday" as preparation for the end of a journey and the beginning of a transition: "True and sincere travelling is no pastime but is as serious as the grave, or any part of the human journey."[52] Like a life, he tells us, a journey should be complete, fulfilled, and honorable and should never be undertaken lightly. There are two journeys in *A Week:* the 1839 travels of Thoreau and his brother and his memory's journey back to that original excursion. Bridging them are the narratives of later excursions made alone after John's death, and all mention the day's end in the west and the coming of night, when no one can travel.

Thoreau also weaves in historical tales—most compellingly, the story of Hannah Dustan, one of the most famous of the seventeenth-century captivity narratives. During King William's War in 1697, the Abenaki raided her village of Haverhill, Massachusetts. Her husband and eight of her children managed to escape, but Hannah, her infant, and a nurse, Mary Neff, were captured. Before marching them north, the Indians bashed the infant's head against an apple tree. Hannah and Mary were taken to an island at the mouth of the Merrimack River where they were joined by fourteen-year-old Samuel Lenderson. One night, while their captors were sleeping, Hannah, Mary, and Samuel killed nine of them with tomahawks. Before escaping down the river to freedom, Hannah decided they should collect the scalps of the murdered Abenaki, not only as proof of what they had done but also in order to collect the bounty.

In "Thursday," Thoreau first mentions autumn toward the end of Dustan's story. As the scholar H. Daniel Peck has noted, at this point "the narration shifts abruptly into the present, as the historical time of Henry Thoreau and Hannah Dustan conflate, . . . creating the effect that Thoreau and his brother John have joined Hannah's party and are participating in its flight."[53] What the brothers are fleeing is historical time, moving with Dustan into Thoreau's mythology of timelessness. The writer chooses compelling details as he shows the party returning to the scene of the massacre to take the scalps: "They are thinking of the dead they left behind . . . and of the relentless living warriors who are in pursuit."[54] In a way, the scene parallels the surviving brother's story: he, too, has been moving against the current as he retrieves the dead from obscurity. Like the Thoreau brothers, Hannah and her companions pass innumerable graves—Indian graves, mostly vanished by 1839. The scene's most startling image, and one Thoreau returns to, centers on the apple tree on which the infant's "brains [were] dashed out." The surviving members of the family reassemble there, and "there have been many who in later times have lived to say they have eaten the fruit of this apple tree."[55]

After a break in the prose, Thoreau continues, "This seems a long while ago, yet it happened since Milton wrote his Paradise Lost."[56] In this way he connects the apple tree in Hannah's story with the Tree of Knowledge in Eden. As the scholar Steven Fink notes, "[Hannah and her companions] reached their homes with their trophies, but the bloodstained apple tree stands as an emblem of the Fall, and subsequent generations have continued to eat of its fruit."[57] Thoreau's concern here is not sin but its consequences—death and the knowledge of death. Hannah becomes one in a chain of Eves stretching from the beginning of time to the moment of Thoreau's remembrance: "Taking hold of hands they would span the interval from Eve to my own mother. A respectable tea party merely—whose gossip would be Universal History."[58] By domesticating death, he is once again naturalizing it.

Apple trees are everywhere in *A Week,* and their ubiquity is itself a link to dying. In "Sunday," Thoreau talks of the farmer who first "planted orchard seeds brought from the old country, and persuaded the civil apple tree to blossom next to the wild pine and juniper, shedding its perfume in the wilderness."[59] Yet even though the tree is nourishing, beautiful, and fragrant, those who planted it brought death to the original inhabitants of the region. Now those first farmers are also long dead, and memories of them, like the ruins of their homesteads, are fading into obscurity. Thoreau notes the declivities in the ground where apple trees once grew and tells us that the trees usually outlive many generations of humans. His discussion of apple trees is reminiscent of his many tales of old border characters— the old fisherman in his "naturalized" coat and the old woman—another gossiping Eve—approached by the railroad managers.[60] When they ask her how high she remembers the river to have risen, she goes to an apple tree planted by her ancestors and, with the help of her elderly husband, locates the nail that was driven into its trunk to mark the height of the great flood—another biblical reference. The men do not believe her, but of course she is right, as the next flood proves.[61] At the end of the book, Thoreau mentions the apple tree where the brothers tie up their boat, a tree that was also there at the beginning of their journey.

As Thursday, summer, and the journey draw to a close, Thoreau recalls his earlier image of the figure stepping forward into the mist: "the shore itself, and the distant cliffs, were dissolved by the undiluted air. The hardest material seemed to obey the same law as the most fluid, and so indeed, in the long run it does."[62] The shadowy brother, in this situation, cannot be lost because the whole planet, even as it is most alive, is fading out of sight. The journey on the rivers is a fluid one, and the hardest material—death— obeys fluid laws. Dying naturally rounds out the westward course of living, but anything once living is living still, as Krishna points out to Arjuna in the Bhagavad Gita.[63]

The great moment of transition takes place during the night between Thursday and Friday, when the season changes and Henry prepares to take leave of his brother. As the scholar Robert Milder points out, "The chapter ["Friday"] opens with a change of season . . . that can signal either a reinvigoration of life after the hot, dusty Concord summer, or the incursion of time, history, decay, and death into the travelers' and New England's idyll."[64] The speed of the brothers' return creates an elegiac air, grief over what was so significantly shared between them—their youth. Whenever Thoreau describes his later solitary journeys and makes his solitary speculations, we get the sense of a man now fully grown, alone at Walden, writing the single journal of his remembrance.

Throughout, the exuberant noise of the brothers balances with the silences of solitude and recollection. At the beginning of "Tuesday," the two are up far before dawn, awakening the woods with their loud busyness. As they sail into the locks that will take them back to the Concord River on Friday afternoon, each eating half an apple pie, they overflow with youth and exuberance: "We bounded merrily before a smacking breeze, with a devil-may-care look in our faces."[65] Yet the scene is described without sound, like an old memory or a dream. A few pages earlier, Thoreau both sets up that scene of return and describes his present solitude. Once again the brothers act in tandem—one going ashore to buy the pie from a farmer's wife, the other remaining in the boat. But this time they are separated both temporally and spatially. Their "supply was now exhausted"—a reference to their lost companionship—and Henry, "in the boat which was moored to the shore, [was] left alone to his own reflections."[66]

On Thursday night, as the season is preparing to change and the brothers are preparing for sleep, Thoreau first uses the plural in reference to the diary of their excursion: he says they write in "our journals." In the following paragraph he immediately goes back to his original style, the singular noun *journal,* though he retains the plural pronoun: "Unfortunately, many things have been omitted which should have been included in our journal."[67] After this, he does not mention writing again. His brother's voice has departed from his experience, and the only journal that remains is the book of reconstructive memory he is sharing with his reader. At the same time, he creates a parallel experience in the change of the seasons: "For summer passes into autumn in some unimaginable point in time, like the turning of a leaf."[68]

"Friday" introduces autumn with a prophecy of the winter to come: "We fancied by the faces of men that the Fall had commenced," followed by "In all the woods the leaves were fast ripening for their fall . . . and we knew that the maples, stripped of their leaves among the earliest, would soon stand like a wreath of smoke along the edge of the meadow."[69] His use of "we" is particularly interesting here. The choice makes the brothers complicit in the knowledge that one of them, like summer, is dying and the other, like the seasons to come, is still living. In a mediation on thinking and poetry, Thoreau continues to elegize his brother: "Great men, unknown to their generation, have their fame among the great who have preceded them, and all true worldly fame subsides from their highest estimate beyond the stars."[70] Here, he puns on "fame," which had two meanings in the nineteenth century: the one we are accustomed to and, more simply, a man's good name. A man's good name precedes him before and after history. Thus, if fame is acknowledged greatness of achievement, it can only be truly known by the ages. The implication is that through the writer's own knowledge and his shared memorializing, such fame belongs to both brothers.

At this point in the chapter, Thoreau introduces a poem, "The Poet's Delay," whose middle stanza reads:

> Amidst such boundless wealth without,
> I only still am poor within,
> The birds have sung their summer out,
> But still my spring does not begin.[71]

Who has just experienced the seasonal change? It seems that Thoreau has gained his knowledge through the shared consciousness with his brother, even though he writes in the voice of the single poet, the voice of "my journal." With his brother as muse, however, he will continue into the cycle of his own new year.

Thoreau writes, "The places where we had stopped or spent the night on our way up the river had already acquired a slight historical interest for us."[72] "Slight" is an understatement, for the whole book has involved the placement of the brothers in history. They are now embedded in the most recent layer of the landscape, above the Native Americans, the settlers and the fishermen, and burgeoning industrialization. His use of "we" is again interesting because it seems to imply a final backward glance at his lost brother. Thoreau goes on to say, "Already the banks and the distant meadows wore a sober and deepened tinge for the September air had shorn them of their summer's pride."[73] The remaining brother, on his way to being alone, has lost his summer's pride too. The youth and sap that flowed through and connected the brothers is slipping away, leaving a sober grown man to take his own place in history, a history that begins with the fall.

The perpetual health of nature is a theme Thoreau continues to reiterate: "Only the convalescent raise the veil of nature. An immortality in his life would confer immortality on his abode. The winds should be his breath, the seasons his moods, and he should impart of his serenity to Nature herself."[74] Immortality inheres in the wind's breath, and the survivor can partake of it if he can match the serenity of the one who is dead but not lost. Autumn, as the writer has demonstrated, has many moods. The very immortality that now defines his brother increases the serenity of nature. Yet as he says in "Friday,"

> The mast is drooping within my woods,
> The winter is lurking within my moods,
> And the rustling of the winter leaf
> Is the constant music of my grief.[75]

After the joyous placement of the brothers in nature, Thoreau still feels grief for his companion's loss. But grief cannot be all-encompassing if it has background music. Perhaps grief and joy are the same music heard differently. Coming from a withered leaf, it is the music of nature. It predicts winter but also the spring that will follow.

As *A Week* draws to a close, the "we" of John and Henry becomes the more universal "we" of Thoreau and his readers: "Thus thoughtfully we were rowing homeward to find some autumnal work to do, and help on the revolution of the seasons."[76] Conscious of the fall from both grace and youth, Thoreau still finds hope in the cyclical movement of nature. Morning work is preceded by autumnal work, and merging with nature makes living a form of moving time.

Though both brothers participate in the action of "Friday," John's presence notably diminishes. John exists in the summer of experience, but in autumn he can only be remembered. Thoreau describes that autumn as full of movement and energy, the richest time of the year, yet also tinged with dying: "[We saw] by the hue of the grapevine, the goldfinch on the willow, the flickers flying in flocks, and when we passed near enough to see the shore, by the faces of men, that the Fall had commenced."[77] In this passage he uses "Fall" instead of "autumn," a word choice that resonates with his earlier reference to *Paradise Lost.* When he writes, "Our thoughts, too, began to rustle," the "our" is not just Henry and John; all of humankind is partaking in the restlessness that precedes death.[78]

Thoreau emphasizes the elegiac purpose of "Friday" by noting the return of summery weather as the brothers begin rowing up the Concord River. The weather implies a kind of Indian-summer nostalgia, emphasizing that, in the narrative of remembrance, only one brother can come back. Describing the pair's tandem activity, he says, "When one landed to stretch his limbs by walking, he soon found himself falling behind his companion," reminding us that Henry has been left behind by John's flight from the world.[79] At the end, however, Henry, rather than John, leaves the boat for the shore, and John, in the boat, slips out of Henry's grasp. The dead are in some measure lost to us. "This is his grief. Let him turn which way he will, it falls opposite to the sun; short at noon, long at eve. Did you ever see it?"[80]

One of the most famous passages in *Walden* occurs in "Spring." It is the description of a merlin hawk, which is often taken as a description of Thoreau himself: "It sported with proud reliance in the fields of air . . . it appeared to have no companion in the universe—sporting there alone— and to need none but the morning and the ether with which it played."[81] A corresponding description of bird imagery appears at the end of *A Week:* "Two herons . . . with their long and slender limbs revealed against the sky—their lofty and silent flight, as they were wending their way at evening, surely not to alight in any marsh on the earth's surface, but perchance on the other side of the atmosphere."[82] The herons are as united as the hawk is solitary. The significant difference is that the hawk never lands but remains in the air. The herons do have a destination, though it does not exist in the temporal world. Rather, they are "bound to some northern meadow."[83] Their union is as inexplicable as their destination: "they are a symbol for the ages to study, whether impressed upon the sky, or sculptured amid the hieroglyphics of Egypt."[84] The dead are everywhere around us but are always a mystery to be contemplated, a memory to be summoned. The elusiveness of the dead corresponds to the elusiveness of time. They exist on the other side of the atmosphere, behind the fog that envelops the mountains and rivers. The story of the dead brother can never be completely told. We are left only with the narrative of "I," the voice of the one left behind, and that, too, is a temporal voice.

Near the end of the book, Thoreau offers a meditation on silence. While he is referring to the silence of death, he also addressing the idea of anticipation. In music, as he knew, anticipation lies in the pause between notes. In a December 1841 Journal entry, written just before his brother's death, he muses, "Death is that expressive pause in the music of the blast."[85] Silence anticipates sound. "If [the writer] makes his volume a mole whereon the waves of silence can break, it is well."[86] Sound and silence encompass one another in the revolution of the seasons, one anticipating the other. If one brother is made silent, the other becomes sound for both of them. "A man may run on confidently for a time, thinking he has . . . [silence] under his thumb, and shall one day exhaust her, but he too must at last be made silent, and men remark only what a brave beginning he made." The past tense of "made" once again links silence to death. All people die and become silent, but even that silence anticipates new music.

The final paragraph of *A Week* narrates the homecoming. The brothers land their boat in the dark, fastening it to a wild apple tree "whose bark still wore the mark which its chain had worn in the chafing of the spring freshets."[87] The cycles of one year and one life draw to a close, but this year's freshets anticipate next year's freshets. We are left imagining the two brothers tying their boat to the apple tree and then climbing up the bank into the shadows.

2

"I did not cry"

The Sentimental Narrative

This evidence of forethought, this simple *reflection* in a double sense of the term, in this flower affecting to me—as if it
said to me Even I am doing my appointed work in the world
faithfully. Not even I however obscurely I may grow amid the
loftier & more famous plants—shirk my work—humble weed
though I am—not even when I have blossomed and lost my
painted petals & am preparing to die down to its root do I forget to fall with my arms around my babe—that the infant may
be found preserved in the arms of its frozen mother.

—HENRY DAVID THOREAU, Journal, August 30, 1851

I

Though Thoreau often judged antebellum society harshly, he was anything
but a hard man. He had a gentle side, and his writings often use the sentimental tropes of popular culture in interesting and novel ways, particularly
in relation to dying.[1] He conceived of heaven as an idealized version of
nature, just as the heaven of the Unitarians and other liberal Protestants
offered an idealized version of middle-class life. He also manipulated other
sentimental tropes, including boyhood, bachelorhood, the hearth, and
domesticity. As the scholar Joanne Dobson notes, "a number of canonical
authors, including Emily Dickinson, Nathaniel Hawthorne, and Herman
Melville, can be seen to participate—in often unrecognized ways—in the
sentimental literary tradition."[2] I add Henry Thoreau to this list.

There was a deep connection between sentimental literature and sentimental culture in the antebellum period. In the 1970s, feminist critics

began reclaiming this literature, but their slant didn't take sentimental culture into account and therefore did not address the intense emotionality the literature evoked. Many academics seem to appreciate the sentimental only if they can read a subversive subtext into it but cannot accept it for its own sake—as an era's usual way of experiencing separation and dying. But Dobson reminds us that "literary Sentimentalism . . . is premised on an emotional and philosophical ethos that celebrates human connection, both personal and communal, and acknowledges the shared devastation of affectional loss."[3] For example, she considers the "sentimental keepsake," which "embodies the memory of love [and] the anguish of separation. . . . The keepsake tradition inscribed an ethos of human connection and separation personally and politically powerful and sufficiently rich to complicate, and even rival, the long acknowledged individualist trope of the American isolato."[4] Thoreau, long considered one of the great nineteenth-century American isolatos, actively participated in of the keepsake tradition. On the last morning of his life, he asked his sister Sophia to give Edmund Hosmer, the friend who had been sitting up with him all night, his own private copy of *A Week on the Concord and Merrimack Rivers*. It had a lock of his brother John's hair pinned to the flyleaf, "which today is as black and glossy as it was then," wrote Hosmer's granddaughter seventy years later.[5]

In an untitled head-note poem in *A Week,* Thoreau makes one of his earliest references to heaven:

> Where're thou sail'st who sailed with me,
> Though now thou climbest loftier mounts,
> And fairer rivers dost ascend,
> Be thou my Muse, my Brother—.[6]

In Thoreau's rendering, heaven holds rarefied versions of the nature the brothers had known together. The mountains are "loftier," the rivers "fairer." And just as the angel brother climbs higher into the heavenly mountains, he ascends, rather than descends, the rivers. When Thoreau asks John to be his muse, he intimates that his brother may also be his guide when he, too, makes those ascents.

A number of years after John's death, Thoreau wrote in his Journal, "I have heard my brother playing on his flute."[7] The use of the present perfect is intriguing. Is he simply referring to a time in the past when he heard his brother play, or is the flute that Thoreau plays his brother's? Is this present, remembered, or heavenly music? One could say that it is all three. Thoreau may be playing his brother's flute and, in doing so, remembers hearing his brother play. Remembered music is like an echo between what is and what is not sound. The sound of his brother playing the flute, however that sound is summoned, may come from a great distance, perhaps from beyond the recognized earthly realm.

John Thoreau, Jr., was the only human who held a place in his brother's heaven. For Thoreau, heaven was primarily the realm to which elements of nature repaired after death. In his Journal he writes about a freshwater clam that some animal has eaten. After the clam's death, its shell's "beauty beams forth and it remains a splendid cenotaph to its departed tenant, symbolical of those radiant realms of light to which [the clam] has risen,—what glory he has gone to."[8] Likewise, in "Chesuncook," a chapter of *The Maine Woods,* he writes that the pine tree he admires will perhaps reach heaven just as he will, "there to tower above me still."[9] In other words, Thoreau imagines a hierarchical heaven similar to the one described in Elizabeth Stuart Phelps's *The Gates Ajar* (1865) or George Woods's *The Gates Wide Open* (1869).[10] Though Thoreau's heaven doesn't contain pianos and good things to eat, saintly mothers or assassinated presidents, it is a perfected but recognizable world, and one he refers to often.

Thoreau brings up the idea of heaven in both of the pond chapters in *Walden.* In "The Pond in Winter," he sends his beloved pickerel there: "Easily, with a few convulsive quirks, they give up their watery ghosts, like a mortal translated before his time to the thin air of heaven."[11] His use of the Puritan idea of translation is interesting and suggests that his views on heaven evolved after his brother's death. In *A Week* he talks about the violent deaths in nature, the "incessant tragedies," and says of the fallen animals that "none are translated."[12] The Christian idea that heaven was established with the translation of Jesus seems to have been transmuted here: heaven came into existence with the translation of his brother, and now all of nature goes to join John as it is translated. The purity of the Walden water is also analogous to heaven. In "The Ponds," he looks down on Walden from the slight elevation of his house site, an act that reminds him of looking down on the sky from a heavenly home: "It is remarkable that we can look down on [Walden's] surface. We shall, perhaps, look down thus on the surface of air at length and mark where a still subtler spirit sweeps over it."[13]

II

Thoreau's rare writings about his own boyhood are evocative. In "The Bean-Field," another chapter from *Walden,* he evokes the memory of seeing the pond for the first time, when he was four years old. His family had come from Boston to Concord, Henry's birthplace, to visit his maternal grandmother and, while they were there, took a wagon to the pond for a picnic. He recalls the memory as one of his earliest, saying, "And now tonight my flute has awakened the echoes over the water." His visual memory is also a kind of echo: "The pines still stand here, older than I, or if some have fallen I have cooked my supper with their stumps, and a new growth is rising all around, preparing another aspect for new infant eyes."[14] In this lovely passage he creates a continuity among past, present, and future, building a scene that is both enduring and in flux. The fallen trees introduce dying into the child's paradise; yet as nature's representatives, their dying precipitates new life. The aspect may be similar when future children experience it, who will perhaps alter the landscape as he does with his beans.

In his essay "Huckleberries," Thoreau recalls himself as ten-year-old boy who not only absorbs scenes but has agency of his own. On a summer morning, the Thoreau women decide to make a huckleberry pudding for a dinner guest, and Henry is sent off to the hills to gather the berries. "My rule in such cases was never to eat one until my dish was full, for going a-berrying implies more than eating the berries." Though playful, this passage links the experience of loss to the task of gathering wild berries. On one level, it makes a humorous reference to "going a-blackberrying"—that is, going to the devil.[15] But at a deeper level, the task becomes a metonym for the experience of boyhood, for "they at home got nothing but the pudding, a comparatively heavy affair."[16] A pudding for dinner cannot compare to the lightness of a morning spent in the August sunshine. Filling his dish is a kind of tithing for adulthood; the berries he eats afterward are all his own. Their taste mirrors the solitary joy of the boy on the hillside, and the berries themselves symbolize the gift of a pure and complete relation to nature. Yet the act of calling up this recollection highlights the fact that this particular boy now exists only in memory.

Biographers have collected anecdotes of Thoreau's childhood that have come down to us through local recollections. Many involve mishaps. His aunt Sarah Thoreau taught him to walk, and "he was tossed by a cow when he played near the door in a red flannel dress." While living in Chelmsford between the ages of one and three, he chopped off his toe with an ax. Once he fell downstairs and lost consciousness. "'It took two pails of water to bring me to,' he boasted, 'for I was remarkable for holding my breath in those cases.'" There is also an interesting tale about a conversation he had with his mother. Noticing that he was still awake in the trundle bed next to his sleeping brother, she asked, "'Why Henry dear don't you go to sleep?' 'Mother,' he replied, 'I have been looking through the stars to see if I could see God behind them.'" As a grown man he sometimes boasted that when the Reverend Ezra Ripley baptized him, he didn't cry.[17]

Yet even when he is not sharing specific stories of his own childhood, boyhood and its loss are everywhere in his Journal. In his June 9, 1850, entry, Thoreau writes, "My imagination, my love & reverence & admiration, my sense of the miraculous is not so excited by any event as by the remembrance of my youth."[18] That sentiment appears throughout his writings. He has a Wordsworthian sense of childhood but sees growing up as merely a prelude to death. In chapter 1, I discussed his poem "Sympathy," which I read as an elegy to boyhood. He wrote that poem in his early twenties, yet its resonance stayed with him his entire life.

In another June 1850 Journal entry, Thoreau evokes both the sentimental and the pastoral when he describes the boys who are helping their fathers drive milk cows and their calves fifty miles north to summer grazing in New Hampshire. The scene is a direct contrast to the death of pastoralism he describes in *Walden*, when he writes about the railroad in the chapter "Sounds." The drovers leave "early in the morning with their sticks and dogs—it is a memorable time for the farmer boys." When they and their fathers return for the cows in the fall, the boys "speculate whether Janet or brindle will know them—I heard such a boy exclaim on such an occasion when the calf of spring returned a heifer—as he stroked her side—she knows me father—she knows me—Driven up to be cattle on a thousand hills."[19] The poignancy of this beautiful description is tinged with loss. Sending the cattle north in spring leads inevitably to the fall in both senses of the word. The fact that the heifers, no longer calves, have names and "know me" emphasizes the boys' individuality even as it suggests that the experience is universal. Thoreau shifts from the plural "boys"—will the cows know *them?*—to a specific boy, who is sure that the heifer "knows me." "Driven up to be cattle on a thousand hills,"[20] these cows become the herd that descends on the railroad in *Walden*. Just as the individual family animals become "cattle," the farm boy grows out of his particularity and becomes another adult among many—a kind of dying. The solitary journal keeper can only record and re-create the boy's vanished experience.

III

Thoreau didn't follow the common course when he grew out of boyhood; he never married or had a home of his own. Even the small house he built at Walden Pond and lived in for two years was on Emerson's land. As he grew older, the idea of a hearth and a family of his own became ever more untenable. According to his sister Sophia, he spoke of Ellen Sewell as he lay dying, telling Sophia he "had always loved her," though one could argue that he never pursued her very arduously.[21] Nor did he ever pursue another relationship; a single archetypal romance seemed to fulfill his imagination enough to require no sequel.

There is no evidence that family or friends tried to convince Thoreau to marry. In fact, some, such as Emerson, took the opposite tack and argued in favor of bachelorhood. In his essay, "Fireside Chastity: The Erotics of Sentimental Bachelorhood in the 1850s," Vincent J. Bertolini asserts that the bachelor identity could present itself as a cover for "anti-domestic male sexuality."[22] Thoreau's position, however, was just the opposite; in his life at Walden and beyond, he constructed an anti-sexual male domesticity. He put this domesticity into practice in 1847–48, when he lived with Lidian Emerson and her children while Emerson was lecturing abroad for nine months. In November 1847, he wrote to Emerson, "Lidian and I make very good housekeepers. She is a dear sister to me." In this perfect domesticity, Thoreau was not tied down, and the brother-sister bond between Lidian and himself was asexual. But buried in the middle of the same letter was news of a "tragedy." Sophia Ford (sometimes spelled "Foord"), the teacher of the Emerson and Alcott children, had written to him and proposed marriage. He told Emerson, "Of course I did not write a deliberate answer. How could I deliberate upon it? I sent back as distinct a *no* as I have learned to pronounce after considerable practice." Emerson responded, "It is one of the best things connected with my coming hither is that you would & could keep the homestead, that fireplace shines all the brighter,—and has a permanent glitter therefor." He briefly but vehemently mentioned the proposal: "You tell me in your letter of one odious circumstance, which we will dismiss from remembrance henceforward."[23]

It is hard to determine why this proposal so offended Emerson. Ford was a good deal older than Thoreau, but Emerson's own grandmother had been ten years older than her husband, Ezra Ripley. Nineteenth-century women certainly weren't in the habit of proposing to men, not even if they belonged to progressive groups such as the transcendentalists. Yet though either of these factors may have influenced Emerson's response, I think his primary concern was the idea that "my brave Henry," whom he later eulogized as "the bachelor of nature," would compromise his stoic asexuality. Emerson preferred Thoreau to be a brother to his own wife than the husband of another woman.[24]

Any discussion of Thoreau's bachelor status must necessarily consider the influence of Ik Marvel (Donald G. Mitchell), a popular author who was arguably the most famous bachelor in nineteenth-century America. His *Reveries of a Bachelor,* first published in 1850, went through numerous editions and was still widely read by 1900.[25] In that book, an unattached young man sits by a series of firesides, imagining courtship, marriage, family, and dying as he gazes into the flames. It is a fascinating little book, focusing in particular on the liminal status of bachelors in the antebellum period.

Like Marvel, Thoreau describes fireside reveries that end in dying, notably in the *Walden* chapter "Former Inhabitants and Winter Visitors." Whereas each of Marvel's reveries ends with a drawn-out deathbed episode, Thoreau matter-of-factly reports on how the families who lived in Walden Woods died out. Yet his storytelling is as poignant as Marvel's and in this sense fits the mode of the sentimental narrative, though he does avoid Marvel's maudlin imagery. Unlike Marvel, however, he never imagines courtship or marriage: there are families in his reveries but no love interests. His fantasies may all lead to death and dying, but they are assertively non-masturbatory.

Thoreau was certainly anxious about purity, as both his Journal and the *Walden* chapter "Higher Laws" make clear. At the same time, his writings show that he was also aware of the transgressive position of the bachelor in antebellum culture. A bachelor had the potential to live out his sexuality through masturbation, the services of a prostitute, or the unnamed sin we know as homosexuality, and he had the potential of being procreative outside the sanctioned bonds of marriage. In the sentimental narrative, however, none of these frightening possibilities exist for the old maid; like Thoreau, she remains unimpeachably celibate her entire life. Thoreau played this old-maid role in his relations with the Emersons and his own family and in his feminine self-characterizations in *Walden*.

Nonetheless, some of Thoreau's neighbors saw his move to the pond as transgressive, as he humorously shows in the *Walden* chapter "Economy." Wasn't he lonely? they asked suspiciously. Thoreau's emphasis on purity demonstrates his awareness of the masturbation issue behind this interest in his loneliness. The historian Russ Castronovo writes, "Breeding fears about the unsupervised habits of solitary citizens, the discourse against masturbation conflicts with the agendas of self-culture which encouraged young men to discard allegiances to dead institutions and live according to the rhythms of nature, as Thoreau did at Walden."[26]

Combating these fears, Thoreau portrays a busily breeding and procreative earth in which all nature is concurrently mating, dying, and being born, and integrates himself as the solitary, celibate witness. Animals share his house, but nature respects and adorns his yearning toward purity. Of the autumn wasps, he writes, "They never molested me seriously, though they bedded with me."[27] He differs here from Marvel, whose peripatetic character inhabits different spaces for each reverie, including one he shares with a maiden aunt. Marvel spins his reveries over expanses of space and time, while Thoreau sits by the same fire in the same house and evokes the past inhabitants of the space he now occupies. All of Marvel's reveries begin with the same transgressive solitary bachelor and lead to love, families, and dying; Thoreau's begin with already formed families in which the narrator has no role. The only exception to this family paradigm is his tale of an old man so tragically addled by alcoholism as to no longer fit the character of the masturbatory transgressive.

According to the scholars Mary Chapman and Glenn Hendler, the major tropes of sentimental literature are "the dying child, the destruction of families by death, slavery, poverty, and intemperance, and the unnecessary suffering of marginalized figures."[28] Thoreau uses such tropes in "Former Inhabitants." As winter closes in and his visitors dwindle, he enjoys many evenings by his fireside. "For human society I was obliged to conjure up the former inhabitants of these woods." All have died—some long ago, some just before his arrival. "Within memory of many of my townsmen the road near where my house stands resounded with the laugh and gossip of inhabitants, and the woods which bordered it were dotted here and there with their little gardens and dwellings."[29] "Little" is always a key sentimental metonym for Thoreau. The diminutive is not dismissive (his own house is small) but implies unspoiled innocence. He refers to the road through Walden Woods as "a humble route to neighboring villages."[30] Like "little," "humble" connotes a harmless people who lead simple lives and don't deserve their sad fates. Even though Thoreau often tells us he is happy to be the solitary human inhabitant of the woods, his descriptions of the former inhabitants show his compassion for the loss, suffering, and dying that made his solitude possible.

In *Black Walden: Slavery and Its Aftermath in Concord, Massachusetts*, Elise Lemire reminds us that the true story of the freeing of the slaves during and after the American Revolution does not match the antebellum abolitionist narrative. Rather, "many of the slaveholders [in Concord] decided to abandon their slaves to freedom. . . . Unable to purchase land, these abandoned slaves were permitted to squat locally, but only on the most out-of-the-way abandoned places." Walden Woods was one of those sites; others were "the swampy edge of the town's Great Field" and a patch of infertile land near the Old Marlborough Road purchased by an ex-slave from Virginia (Elisha Dugan's father). Poor soil quality in all of these locations made it "impossible for the former slaves to rise out of poverty." The Walden community was the shortest lived of the three black settlements. "After forty years of struggling and largely failing to adequately feed their families, the black community at Walden ceased to exist." The other two communities lasted longer, due to the slightly better quality of the soil, but after nearly a hundred years, they were gone too. "The children of these black enclaves who did not die of malnutrition left town."[31]

The first of the former slaves Thoreau mentions is Cato Ingraham, whose former master had built him a cabin in Walden Woods. Cato tended a small plot of early-maturing walnut trees, whose wood and nuts he had hoped to use as a cash crop—like Henry's beans—to support his family in the future, but his plans came to nothing. Thoreau shows us Cato's cellar hole, filled with sumac and luxuriant goldenrod, as if it were a grave ornamented with wildflowers.[32] Lemire writes:

> Cato Ingraham died [of consumption] in the summer of 1805, ten years after arriving in Walden Woods. His daughter Nancy died three months

later at [age] sixteen, having contracted the infection from her father while caring for him. With her passing, the entire Ingraham family was gone, wiped out after the short span of eight months. Henry knew enough of their story that he was moved to note of Cato's walnut trees, that "a younger and whiter speculator got them at last" . . . The valuable trees [had been] planted as an investment in a future that never arrived for his family.[33]

Thoreau also mentions Zilpa, another former slave, whose real name was Zilpah White. Lemire tells us,

In every way Zilpah White was a very unusual woman by Concord standards. Unlike so many former slave women, she shunned the de facto slavery of live-in domestic servitude and spun her way [she had somehow acquired a spinning wheel] to an independent living. Supplementing her meager income from this pre-industrial skill with basket making and other Native American crafts, and readily accepting whatever charity she could get, Zilpah was able to live on her own for over forty years, a feat matched by no other Concord woman of her day.[34]

Although Thoreau doesn't tell us she rebuilt her cabin after the British burned it (along with her animals and her spinning wheel) during the War of 1812, we do know that he saw her fate as a sentimental tragedy. Over "her gurgling pot," he writes, she would declare, "Ye are all bones, bones!" All she left behind, he notes, are "bricks and an old oak copse."[35]

Brister Freeman was another character in *Walden*. He was well known in Concord and was frequently harassed. He changed his last name from Cummings, his old master's last name, to Freeman when he enlisted in the Continental Army for the third time.[36] After his wife died, he shocked the white population by marrying a white woman. Brister grew apple trees on the scrap of land he owned in Walden Woods, some of which Thoreau was able to sample, finding them "wild and ciderish to my taste."[37] This description hints at poverty and suffering, yet elsewhere Thoreau often declares he prefers the taste of wild apples. Thus, his wording implies a kinship between the two men. Thoreau writes about Brister's tombstone in Lincoln, which describes him as "'a man of color' as if he were discolored."[38] Once again, Thoreau makes it clear that he distrusts all tombstones: this one tells only "when he died, which was but an indirect way of telling me he had ever lived." The only meaningful monument exists in those "wild and ciderish" apples.

"With [Brister] dwelt Fenda, his hospitable wife, who told fortunes, yet pleasantly."[39] Lemire notes that "telling fortunes [was] similar to weaving baskets insofar as it required little or no capital to get started in business . . . It is possible, too, that Fenda, who seems to have been born in Africa, if her dark skin and African name are any indication, drew on her experiences with indigenous sub-Saharan African version of fortune telling."[40] By linking together Fenda and Brister in his narrative, Thoreau creates a family, and he suggests that her "pleasant" fortune telling dwelt on the hopes and longings of her customers rather than on their fears. Most significant is the assertion that she was "hospitable." By showing this poor person's kindness to neighbors and customers, he creates a sense of warmth and community, making its dying out more tragic.

Lemire writes, "As Henry takes pains to explain . . . Walden Woods [was] not exclusively the home of former slaves. Rather, the former slaves clustered together within a larger enclave of other poor inhabitants who in two cases were outcasts on account of being alcoholics in addition to being impoverished. John Breed was said to charge six cents for a haircut when he was desperate to buy a drink."[41] Thoreau begins his complicated story of "Breed's location" with a well-known temperance homily in which rum, disguised as a friend and a helper, leads a family to ruin.[42] According to tradition, a tavern once stood on that spot, but Thoreau doesn't clarify whether the Breeds were the owners or just the hapless customers. Humorously interjecting himself into the story, he tells us that he is nodding off over his studies one evening when he is roused by the fire bell. He joins the slapstick chase of men and boys in search of the fire; but when they discover it, they decide it is too far advanced for them to do anything but stand around and watch it burn.

A tragic note enters the tale when Thoreau finds himself in the same location the following night. In a dreamlike encounter, he meets "the only survivor of the family that I know heir to both its virtues and vices, who alone was interested in this burning, lying on his stomach and looking over the cellar wall at the still smoldering cinders beneath, muttering to himself." The man had been working nearby and had returned to the home of "his fathers" only to find it destroyed. The family itself had already been wiped out by drink, and this last pathetic figure, lingering at the smoking ruins of his childhood home, is a character straight out of domestic fiction. He lies there staring at the ruins as though looking for "some treasure"—by implication, his family, his younger self, a time when he and his loved ones still had hope. He is comforted by Thoreau's presence and shows him "where the well was covered up, which, thank heaven, could never be burned, and he groped about for the well-sweep his father had cut . . . I felt it and still remark it almost daily in my walks for on it hangs the history of a family."[43]

Thoreau also writes about John Wyman, a potter, who was the father of another potter, Thomas Wyman. According to Lemire, Thomas "was somehow able to purchase land in Walden and it is from him that Ralph Waldo Emerson purchased the eleven acres on which Henry began to squat in 1845."[44] We learn from Thoreau that Hugh Quoil (actually spelled Quoyle) squatted in Thomas Wyman's hut after Wyman's death and was believed to have been a British war hero at Waterloo. If this tale is true, then he lived a life of great irony. According to Thoreau, Quoil could behave like a gentleman, but he had declined into the final phases of alcoholism. Red-faced, "he wore a greatcoat in mid-summer being affected with the trembling delirium." Like John Breed, he died in the road: "All I know of him is tragic." The writer visits Quoil's hut before it is torn down and inventories his few sad and tattered belongings. His unhoed garden is overgrown, and "the skin of a woodchuck was freshly stretched to the back of the house, a trophy of his last Waterloo, but no warm cap or mittens would he want more."[45]

Thoreau sums up the former inhabitants by describing the small indentations in the earth that mark their cellar holes as well as the trees that have sprung up where the front doors may have been. "Sometimes the well-dent is visible where a spring once oozed . . . What a sorrowful act that must be—the covering up of wells! coincident with the opening of the wells of tears. These cellar dents . . . are all that is left where once were the stir and bustle of human life." More sentimentally, he muses on the lilacs still growing next to where the doors once stood. He introduces children—black children—for the first time in the chapter, imagining that each lilac "[unfolds] its sweet-smelling flowers every spring . . . planted and tended once by children's hands . . . Little did the dusky children think that the puny slip . . . [would] tell their story faintly to the lone wanderer half a century after they had grown up and died."[46] Thoreau concludes the section by rhetorically asking why this "small village, germ of something more," did not survive. He knows the answer: the soil was poor, the people were poor, many were black, and all were dogged by tragedy.

Interestingly, Thoreau peoples the second half of the chapter with his own visitors, once again filling the woods with laughter and gossip. The bridge between the two sections is his detailed description of a dozing barred owl, which recalls Thoreau's own fireside reveries. It also reminds us that he and his visitors, like the former human inhabitants, will also vanish. (In fact, he was already gone when he wrote this chapter.) Only nature is constant.

In his discussion of the former inhabitants, Thoreau repeatedly describes the luxuriance of the wild plants growing in the cellar holes as if the former inhabitants gave even greater extravagance to the nature they had died into. Though he asks to be delivered from cities built on the ruins of cities, he has just spent half a chapter describing the ruins amid which his house stands. Likewise, he tells us earlier, in "The Bean-Field," that he often hoes up Native American tools and arrowheads, artifacts of an even older civilization. He leaves us to resolve such paradoxes on our own and ends his section on the former inhabitants by saying, "With such reminiscences I lulled myself to sleep."[47] By calling his reveries "reminiscences," he collapses the time between his life in the woods and the lives of those now dead. His reminiscences, like Marvel's reveries, keep him company on cold nights. Yet unlike Marvel's, his dead are not stereotypes but real people who struggled, suffered, and died too soon.

IV

When Thoreau's sister Sophia sold the family house to the Alcotts and moved to Maine in 1872, she left most of the family's possessions, including Henry's, to the Concord antiquarian Cummings E. Davis, whose collections Henry had admired and contributed to during his life. The items were eventually donated to the Concord Antiquarian Society, now the Concord Museum.[48] Among Thoreau's possessions in that collection is a china figurine that may seem incongruous with our contemporary conceptions of him. The ten-inch-tall piece is a representation of Uncle Tom and Little Eva, characters in Harriet Beecher Stowe's novel *Uncle Tom's Cabin.* According to Sophia, a fugitive slave whom Thoreau had helped escape to Canada later sent it to him in gratitude. The man's name is unrecorded.

The works of Stowe and Thoreau share a number of motifs—for instance, the centrality of fire and the hearth. In sentimental literature, the open hearth often represents family closeness and emotional and physical comfort; but burning through that benignity is always the idea of loss and dying. For instance, in her novels *The Minister's Wooing* (1859) and *Oldtown Folks* (1869), Stowe laments the passing of the huge open kitchen fireplaces of pre-industrial New England. Both books devote many pages to loving descriptions of these old fireplaces, which ran the length of a wall, were built up with tree-sized logs, and included nooks where family and friends could rest, drink cider, and tell old stories.

In the years after the Civil War, rapid geographical expansion began reducing New England's intellectual and cultural primacy in the United States. One response was a deep nostalgia for the "old ways," particularly among regional writers such as Stowe. Yet she also understood that a human presence in nature could be damaging; as Lawrence Buell points out in *The Environmental Imagination,* Thoreau was not the only midcentury advocate for the preservation of New England's forests. The fireplace scenes in *Oldtown Folks* reveal some of Stowe's ambivalence about the past. For instance, one passage describes not only the massive logs used in such fireplaces but also the family's arguments about the best way to construct a fire, juxtaposing comforts with ungodly traits: "There is no little nook of domestic life that gives such snug harbor to so much self-will and self-righteousness as the family hearth."[49] Likewise, in a later chapter, she interrupts a nostalgic woodcutting scene to lament the loss incurred by "the prodigality which fed our great roaring winter fires on those thousand-leafed oaks whose conception had been years ago—who were the children of light and of day—every fibre and fragment of them made of the most celestial influences, of sunshine and rain-drops, and night-dews and clouds, slowly working for centuries until they had wrought the wondrous shape into a gigantic miracle of beauty."[50]

The "Housewarming" chapter of *Walden* expresses a similar duality. One may read the coming of the cold months, when most people stay home in the village rather than visit him by the pond, as the ingathering of Thoreau's domesticity. He emphasizes that he uses only deadfall and stumps for firewood.[51] Nonetheless, his presence in the woods diminishes and changes the landscape. Even the deadfall is exhaustible; and to reduce consumption in his second winter, he uses a woodstove because "I did not own the forest."[52] That impending loss intensifies the poignancy of his earlier relationship with fire.

Thoreau shows us that each movement away from the source of fire represents a loss. In November of his first year, he lingers as long as he can on the northeast end of the pond, where the sun reflects from the woods and the stones by the shore. For the rest of his life he referred to this area as "the fireside." "I thus warmed myself by the still glowing embers which the summer, like a departed hunter, had left."[53] The recompense for this loss is his house's open fireplace, which, like the great kitchen hearths in Stowe's novels, becomes a special locus of feeling. He tells us that building his fireplace was the most pleasurable part of completing his house and that he lingered over it.

Loss always inheres with gain in Thoreau's solidly built but temporary home. He tells us that the house, once plastered, no longer pleased his eye as much, though it was now warmer and more comfortable. The open fireplace becomes "a cheerful housekeeper . . . It was I and fire that lived there; and commonly my housekeeper proved trustworthy"—though he also records the occasion when a live spark from his "housekeeper" burns a spot on his bed as big as his hand.[54] One might read a cautionary tale against sexuality in this passage, especially in light of the quest for purity he has just detailed in "Higher Laws." Yet in a larger sense it seems to suggest the ever-present closeness between comfort and living, destruction and dying. For the moment, however, "Housewarming" keeps that inevitability at bay, and Thoreau and his housekeeper-fire expand their Edenic household. Mice, moles, squirrels, and wasps come to settle in his newly plastered home, sharing a bond of creature comfort. They mirror any human family sheltering together against the cold, passing the winter as domestically as the characters in John Greenleaf Whittier's poem "Snowbound" does.

Thoreau ends the chapter with the poem "The Wood-Fire" by Ellen Sturgis Hooper, previously printed in the first number of *The Dial*.[55] It opens, "Never, bright flame, may be denied to me / Thy dear life imaging, close sympathy." As in Stowe's and Thoreau's writings, her open fire mirrors the minds of the human witnesses. However, this ancient union is becoming a memory, vanquished by new, more industrial means of warmth. She mourns,

> Was thy existence then too fanciful
> For life's common light who are so dull?
> Did thy bright gleam mysterious converse hold
> With our congenial souls? secrets too bold?[56]

Thoreau also sees dying and loss not only in the vanishing of the old-fashioned hearth or the destruction of the forests but also in the very wood as it burns.

Thoreau had a long and storied history with fire, and one famous incident took place when he and Edward Hoar went on a fishing expedition to Fair Haven Bay in April 1844.[57] Despite his experience in woodcraft, Thoreau, intending to cook a chowder, started a fire in a tree stump during a very dry spring. A live spark ignited a field of dead grass, and the fire could not be contained. His biographer Walter Harding notes, "More than three hundred acres [of woods] had been burned over and more than two thousand dollars damage done to the properties of A. H. Wheeler, Cyrus Hubbard, and Darius Hubbard."[58] Thoreau wrote about this fire at length in an undated Journal entry composed between May 31, and June 4, 1850. He begins abruptly, "I once set fire to the woods." When he and Hoar realized that they could not control the fast-moving flames, Hoar ran into town for help, and Thoreau labored alone until he was exhausted. Retrospectively, he rationalized, "I have set fire to the forest—but have done no wrong therein—& now it is as if the lightning had done it. These flames are but consuming their natural food." He also points out that sparks from the railroad cause many more woodland fires. Yet he clings to this memory, perhaps because, at the time of his writing, he had been attempting to put out another fire. One June 4, he wrote, "As I was fighting the fire today in the midst of the roaring & crackling for the fire seems to snort like a wild horse—I heard from time to time the dying strain the last sigh, the fine clear shrill scream of agony as if the trees were breathing their last."[59]

These experiences with woodland fires may have informed his own untitled poem in "Housewarming":

> Light-winged smoke, Icarian bird
> Melting thy pinions in thy upward flight
> . . . .
> By night star-veiling, and by day
> Darkening the light and blotting out the sun;
> Go thou my incense upward from this hearth,
> And ask the gods to pardon this clear flame.[60]

The poem not only celebrates fire but mourns and asks forgiveness for the death it has caused. By comparing the smoke to Icarus, the mythical boy who flies too close to the sun, he grieves for the death inherent in the fire's flight to the sky, "melting thy pinions." Because the smoke from his beloved fire blocks the sun and the living light, it is only morally tenable if its existence becomes a religious exercise: that is, if he sacrifices wood on his homemade altar and the incense he sends to the gods begs pardon for the murder his fire has done.

V

In 1852, F. W. Shelton published "On Old Bachelors," a response to Marvel's *Reveries,* in the *Southern Literary Messenger.*[61] A playful look at the stigma attached to bachelorhood, the essay classifies bachelors into four categories: the involuntary, the sentimental, the misogynist, and the stingy. He also notes a primary difference between bachelors and old maids: bachelors choose their single state; old maids are chosen "since God has willed it."[62] This fits with my previous discussion of Thoreau's single status. As his correspondence with Emerson implies, it was not a willful choice but one created, if not by God, then by his own natural condition.

Shelton's description of old maids supports my contentions about Thoreau. Echoing the biblical prophet Isaiah, he says that old maids "bloom solitary in a desert world where they are well-fitted to grace a garden of loveliness." Likewise, Thoreau bloomed into the genius of another man's hearth. As Shelton tells us, "Aunty's" visit inspires joy among the whole family, particularly the children, who greet her noisily and lead her to the hearth, where the fire is burning brightly in anticipation of her visit. She gives the children individual attention and offers little gifts that they treasure all their lives.

As I mentioned in chapter 1, Emerson's youngest child, Edward, wrote a wonderful book in his old age about his own and others' memories of Thoreau. His goal was to show that Thoreau, despite his occasional brusqueness, was "refined, courteous, kind, and humane." In the book, he talks of Thoreau's familiarity with Emerson household: he would arrive unannounced, "[sound] his note in the hall," and all the children would come running to "hug his knees." Still smothered in that embrace, he would make his way to the fireplace, where he would "[sit] down and [tell] stories" of wild animals he had seen that day and "would make our pencils and knives disappear, then redeem them presently from our ears and noses." Afterward, he would fetch an old copper warming pan, fill it with popcorn, and shake it patiently over the fire until the popped kernels overflowed onto the rug.[63]

Thoreau also feminized himself, creating a bridge between his tasks at Walden and the work of housewives in their homes. Note the subtle shift from female to male referents in this passage from "Economy": "At present . . . a good housewife would sweep out the greater part of [this clutter] into the dust hole and not leave her morning's work undone. Morning work! By the blushes of Aurora and the music of Memnon, what should be a man's *morning work* in this world?"[64] Later in *Walden* he compares himself to Hebe, "cupbearer to Jupiter and daughter of Juno and wild lettuce, who had the power of restoring gods and mortal men to the vigor of youth. She was probably the only sound-conditioned, healthy, and robust young lady that ever walked the globe, and wherever she came, it was spring."[65] Hebe is a virgin goddess, the prototypical old maid, and his comparison seems to explain why he has chosen to remain celibate and why his own people will die out with him.

VI

After the death of his brother John in 1842 and his sister Helen in 1849, Thoreau's remaining people included his parents, his sister Sophia, the various single and widowed aunts who often lived with the family, and a narcoleptic bachelor uncle. With the exception of his parents, all remained childless. "Left Mr. Emerson and began living at Father's July 30th, 1848," he wrote on a scrap of paper, possibly excised from his Journal, and he stayed with his family for the rest of his life when he was not traveling or lecturing.[66] In 1850, the family moved to the Yellow House, which Thoreau helped his father renovate. The house was more capacious than any of the family's previous ones, thanks in part to the success of the family's graphite business. Henry had the whole attic to himself, which gave him enough privacy to read and write at home and enough space for his books, his natural history specimens, and his Native American artifacts. Reached by a steep, narrow staircase, the space was double-gabled: on the smaller side was his Spartan sleeping area, on the larger side his study.

Thoreau's return changed his relations with his family. Though individually its members could still exasperate him, he increasingly began to use "we," "us," and "our" when he wrote about family life in his Journal. Next to William Ellery Channing, Sophia became his most frequent boating companion. Watching her son as he nursed his father through his final illness, his mother wrote, " 'If it had not been for my husband's illness, I should never have known what a tender heart Henry had.' "[67] Thoreau shared his intimate musings on boyhood with his family, once leading them to a parlor window to listen to a boy's watermill, which from a distance resembled a tinkling stream. In time, he made so much peace with the family's domestic life that he was able to write nostalgically about going to church, an activity he had renounced at the age of twenty-one. In a June 26, 1852, Journal entry, he recalls bathing in the river on Sunday morning with other young men, and then carry sweet-smelling water lilies to church with them.[68]

Thoreau's writings also domesticate nature. In his Journal, he repeatedly uses words such as "pretty," "little," and "tender" to describe plants, even when he is otherwise scientific. In his view, their vulnerability and loveliness heighten the idea of the willing sacrifice they make to future seasons. He often personifies the seasons, writing of how each dies in turn to make room for the next—most poignantly when he describes the gradual, beautiful dying of winter into a new spring. While he never abandoned the idea of nature as strange and mysterious, he also conceived of it as a growing and dying family.

In the 1851 Journal entry that opens this chapter, I hear an echo of the early nineteenth-century English ballad "Mary of the Wild Moor," which tells the tale of a young mother freezing to death while sheltering her baby from the wind.[69] The ballad was a popular parlor song in the nineteenth-century, and Thoreau may have been familiar with it. But whether or not he knew it, he was familiar with the sentimental idea of motherly self-sacrifice, and his writings apply that trope to dying and rebirth in nature. In *Walden*, he says, "When the ground was partially bare of snow . . . it was pleasant to compare the first tender signs of the infant year just peeping forth with the stately beauty of the withered vegetation that had withstood the winter, . . . decent weeds at least, that widowed nature wears." Continuing, he declares that the beginning of spring makes music from the dying of winter, just as the first birds sing "as if the flakes of winter tinkled as they fell!"[70]

Later in *Walden*, Thoreau again uses the sentimental motifs of motherhood, infancy, and dying. In "Brute Neighbors," after telling us that the phoebe and the robin have built nests near his house for protection, he describes a mother partridge who is "clucking and calling" to her chicks "like a hen." Suddenly aware of a human nearby, she utters "her anxious calls and mewing," drags her wings on the ground, and commences to "roll and spin around in such a dishabille, that you cannot, for a few moments, detect what kind of creature it is."[71] He then turns to sentimental notions of infancy to describe the chicks themselves, applying the Romantic paradigm of the wisdom of infancy. At the warning call of their mother, they scatter and camouflage themselves among the leaves, where they will stay if she is killed until they die themselves. He says he has held single chicks in his hand, and they remain "obedient to their mother and their instinct, . . . squat[ting] there without fear or trembling." Their eyes "suggest not merely the purity of infancy, but a wisdom clarified by experience. Such an eye was not born when the bird was, but is coeval with the sky it reflects."[72]

In a September 8, 1851, Journal entry, Thoreau talks sentimentally about the transitions of the year, this time discussing autumn in words that echo the poet William Cullen Bryant: "May my life not be destitute of this Indian summer . . . when I may once more lie on the ground with faith as in spring—& even with more serene confidence—And then I will [wrap] the drapery of summer about me & lie down to pleasant dreams. So does our life pass into another through the medium of death."[73] Once more he subtly brings up the idea of heaven—or perhaps transmigration—and combines it with the mysticism of transition. The idea of the beautiful death appears often in his Journal. His December 28, 1851, entry considers the winter sky at sunset: "I think you never see such brightness as in the western sky sometimes before the sun goes down in the clouds, like the extasy we [are] told sometimes lights up the face of a dying man—that is a *serene*—or evening death—like the end of the day."[74] Here, he reverses the usual simile: instead of the dying man's face lighting up like the evening sky, the evening sky lights up like a dying man's face. As he did throughout his life, he personifies nature with a sentimental image of dying.

3

Blood and Seeds

The Heroic Narrative

Shall the earth be regarded as a graveyard—a necropolis merely—& not also as a granary filled with the seeds of life? Is
not its fertility increased by this decay? a fertile compost not
exhausted sand.

But hark! I hear the tolling of a distant funeral bell, and they
are conveying a corpse to the churchyard from one of the
houses that I see, and its serious sound is more in harmony
with this scenery than any ordinary bustle could be. It suggests
that a man must die to his present life before he can appreciate
his opportunities and the beauty of the abode that is appointed
him.

—HENRY DAVID THOREAU, Journal, March 11, 1854,
and October 7, 1857

I

As even his earliest writings make clear, Thoreau had heroism on his mind,
and he believed that the true measure of heroism was dying bravely and
cheerfully. His fascination with the heroism of dying manifested itself in his
intense interest in vanishing Native American cultures and his lifelong passion for classical literature. Thomas Carlyle's *On Heroes and Hero Worship
and the Heroic in History* was a major early influence, as his 1843 essay "Sir
Walter Raleigh" demonstrates.[1] As Thoreau matured as a writer, he began
to see nature as the truest exemplar of heroic dying. Four late essays—
"Walking," "Autumnal Tints," "Wild Apples," and "Huckleberries"—arose
from early 1850s Journal entries. Just before his death, he revised the first

three for posthumous publication in the *Atlantic Monthly,* and somewhat earlier he had worked "Huckleberries" into the form of a lecture, culling from an unfinished manuscript, "Notes on Fruit." All four essays eloquently evoke nature in late summer and autumn and anticipate his own dying.

Unlike the late nature essays, which Thoreau composed intermittently over more than a decade, his three John Brown essays were based on Journal entries written between October and December 1859. Yet the heroic dying imagery is remarkably similar in both sets, and the Brown essays also center around the seasons. For instance, Thoreau is aware that Brown's raid, arrest, trial, and execution takes place as autumn dies into winter. For him, Brown was heroic as nature was heroic, and he was devastated that a "whole crop of heroes" did not immediately sprout when Brown and his men were cut down. Though many people believe that Thoreau distanced himself from Brown shortly after the hanging, I believe that the Brown essays and the late nature essays fueled his move toward his last lecture, "The Succession of Forest Trees."

Carlyle's *On Heroes and Hero Worship* was published in the United States in 1841, when Thoreau was twenty-three years old, and it made a huge impression on all of the transcendentalists. John Brown's biographer, David S. Reynolds, posits that the book's resurrection of Oliver Cromwell's reputation made the later deification of John Brown possible: thanks to Carlyle, Americans came to see Brown as Cromwell's successor.[2] Yet the book influenced Thoreau's work long before Brown came onto the scene, moving him to write about Sir Walter Raleigh, one of his favorite English poets, whom he saw as a great, if flawed, hero.

In his Raleigh essay, Thoreau borrows two tropes from Carlyle: first, that a hero's flaws stem from the flawed times in which he lives; second, that his greatness comes from his likeness to nature. The essay points out Raleigh's "somewhat antique Roman virtues," and calls him "one of nature's noblemen. Among savages he still would have been a chief. He seems to have had, not a profounder or grander but . . . more nature than other men."[3] Raleigh was flawed because he was a courtier, betraying his natural self for the niceties and flattery of court life. But as a Carlylian hero, he represented both the worst and best of his "stirring" age. As Thoreau writes, "the discovery of America and the successful progress of the Reformation opened a field for both the intellectual and physical energies of his generation."[4]

Thus, he compliments Raleigh by making the courtier into a hardy American. Yet the word "intellectual" appears ahead of "physical," for Raleigh was not just a soldier, an adventurer, and an explorer. He was also a heroic writer who composed much of his best work while in prison.[5]

Thoreau lingers on both Raleigh's heroic writing and his heroic dying, as he later does in his essays on Brown. While on trial for his life, Raleigh conducted himself with dignity and graciousness. He spent his last night alive writing verses and letters of farewell and moral instruction to his wife. Likewise, before he was executed, Brown wrote eloquently of the inevitability of abolition and composed letters to his wife about the education of their daughters. Brown was noted for his calm poise on the gallows; Raleigh "went to the scaffold, and appeared with such serene countenance so that a stranger could not have told which was the condemned person."[6] Both men shared a connection to husbandry. Brown raised sheep, and Raleigh "first introduced the potato vine from Virginia, and the cherry tree from the Canaries into Ireland, where his garden was."[7] Like Brown, Raleigh also engaged in peaceful and fruitful relations with the Native Americans.

In Carlyle's conception, a hero is the opposite of a skeptic. This emphasis on earnestness spoke to Thoreau, who searched for sincerity in relationships and society. For both writers, heroism was manifested in actions, thought, and morality. In Carlyle's view, "valor is the fountain of pity too—of truth and all that is great and good in a man."[8] His heroic model was Oliver Cromwell, who also inspired John Brown: the abolitionist kept Joel Tyler Headley's *The Life of Oliver Cromwell* on the same shelf as his Bible.[9] Of Cromwell's dying, Carlyle wrote, "The sun was dimmed many a time but the son had not himself grown a dimness. Cromwell's last words, as he lay waiting for death, are those of a Christian heroic man."[10] Carlyle's pun on "sun" and "son" would have resonated with Thoreau; for him, a great man was always likened to a force of nature. The idea of "a Christian heroic man" anticipates Thoreau's own understanding of Brown, who, though a Christian, avoided the Christian hypocrisy that Thoreau had railed against throughout his life. Brown became, to Thoreau, the one contemporary exemplar of a life based on pure Christian idealism.

Thoreau's sense of heroic idealism infiltrated his understanding of Native Americans. In his seminal study, Robert F. Sayre discusses the influence of savagism on Thoreau's conceptions. "As well as providing fatalistic apologetic for white conquest, . . . [savagism] provoked the elegiac impulse.

The Indian, the daemon of the continent, must be studied and honored while he is yet available."[11] This notion of "the Indian," according to Sayre, propagated the myth of the last, lone native hunter saying good-bye to his ancestral lands. Thoreau frequently incorporated this image into his writings, using it as a fact in itself and as a metaphor for nature victimized by a changing landscape and economy.

Sayre discusses the imaginative intersection between classical literature and the idea of the Indian, who evoked "pity and censure" comparable to "the classical tragic emotions of pity and terror . . . Pity was a concession to the Indian's loss of his lands, his ancient customs, and his former grandeur. Censure was an expression of civilized superiority over this dying race."[12] Thoreau often turns to savagism to indicate that the Indian is doomed, but he doesn't see white economic expansionism as superior. Rather, he uses savagism to reinforce his sense of the elegiac, and this form of anticipation as prophecy permeates all four of the late nature essays. For example, in "Walking" he writes of how the increase in public roads facilitates the marking of private property lines, thus making walks across lots and meadows less possible in the future. "Let us improve our opportunities then, before the evil days come."[13]

Thoreau's late writings use seed imagery in both elegies and jeremiads. In "Walking," he says, "The seeds of instinct are preserved under the thick hides of cattle and horses, like seeds in the bowels of the earth, an indefinite period." In the same essay, he prefigures Brown as a kind of John the Baptist, the seed of change: "In such a soil grew Homer and Confucius . . . and out of such a wilderness comes the Reformer eating locusts and wild honey."[14] Writing of a red maple in "Autumnal Tints," he notes that some trees are so beautiful that "their seed [could] be advertised in the market, as well as radishes, if we cared as much about them." The red maple, he says, has "long since ripened its seeds and committed them to the winds."[15] In "Wild Apples" we learn "that between the rocks you see thousands of little trees just springing up between them, with the seed still attached to them."[16] "Huckleberries" begins with a discussion of how people mistakenly refer to some things as "little," others as "great." "The famous California tree is a great thing—the seed from which it sprang up a little thing—scarcely one traveller has noticed the seed at all—and so with all seeds and the origin of things."[17] In "A Plea for Captain John Brown," he writes of his contemporaries who are unmoved by Brown and his compatriots: "Such do not know that like the seed is the fruit, and that in the moral world when good seed is planted, good fruit is inevitable . . . that when you plant or bury a hero, a crop of heroes is sure to spring up."[18] In "The Martyrdom of John Brown" he refers to Brown as the Roman general Agricola and quotes the poet James Shirley: "Only the actions of the just / Smell sweet and blossom in the dust."[19] "The Succession of Forest Trees" is a full-length consideration of seeds and the source of his remark, "I have great faith in a seed."[20]

Blood imagery, often evoked by the colors purple and red, also permeates the late essays, usually as a symbol of nature's fertility. "Autumnal Tints" is full of references to blood. The purple grass "paint[s] the earth with its blush," the ground is "ensanguined," and the sands are "impurpled": "All sap or blood is now wine-colored. At last we have not only the purple sea, but the purple land."[21] In "Wild Apples," cattle redden the tree trunks by rubbing against them, and apples are "freckled or peppered all over the stem side with fine crimson spots."[22] The blossoms in "Huckleberries" are "tinged with red," and entire hillsides are purple with berries.[23] In "A Plea for Captain John Brown," Brown's chosen company members "sealed their contract with their blood." "No doubt," Thoreau tells us, "you can get more in your market for a quart of milk than for a quart of blood, but that is not the market that heroes carry their blood to." He explains that "evil is not merely a stagnation of blood, but a stagnation of spirit." Thus, the effect of Brown's actions on the North has been to infuse "more and more generous blood into her veins and heart."[24] In "The Martyrdom of John Brown," Thoreau links the sentimental with the heroic, repeating the story of the "Boston lady who had recently visited our hero in prison" to mend his saber-torn clothes and, "for a memento, brought home a pin covered with blood."[25] In "The Succession of Forest Trees," he twice uses the image of reddened soil, fertile ground for nature's seeds.[26]

II

In "Walking," Thoreau tells us he rarely takes his walks in the morning but prefers the afternoon: "In my afternoon walk I would fain forget all my morning obligations."[27] The essay begins facetiously, but there is always resonance in his humor. By likening his walk to a crusade, he not only constructs a religious allegory but also suggests his willingness to stroll unconcernedly and heroically out of the world. An early passage echoes the words of both Jesus and Emerson, opening with "If you are ready to leave father, mother, brother and sister, and wife and child and friends" and completing the thought with the idea that a true walk means putting aside the veil of this life and moving willingly into the next: "If you have paid your debts, and made your will, and settled your affairs, and are a free man, then you are ready for a walk."[28]

Thoreau speaks about "morning work" in *Walden* but, as a dying middle-aged man, chooses to embrace the dying of the day.[29] His biographer Robert D. Richardson, Jr., notes, "He felt himself aging. He found it 'ominous' that as he grew older he had more to say about evening, less about morning."[30] Several times in "Walking" he links his walks to the biblical notion of a human's allotted years: "There is in fact a sort of harmony discoverable between the capabilities of the landscape within the circle of ten miles' radius, or the limits of an afternoon walk, and the threescore years and ten of human life."[31] The essay's rhetoric about the westward course of America and civilization may seem patriotic, but Thoreau's patriotism always contains a sting, and his allusions to *west* are always elegiac. He writes, "Columbus felt the westward tendency more strongly than any before. He obeyed it, and found a new world for Castile and Leon."[32] Yet while Emerson saw Christopher Columbus as a representative of the Over-soul's desire to visualize its knowledge, Thoreau has his doubts. His dichotomy of east and west is not so simple.

In "Walking," Thoreau describes two panoramas—one of the Rhine, the other of the Mississippi. Of the Rhine he says, "They were the ruins that interested me chiefly," but of the Mississippi he writes, "The foundations of castles were yet to be laid . . . I felt that *this was the heroic age itself,* though we know it not, for the hero is commonly the simplest and obscurest of men."[33] This remark, with its interesting use of time, echoes Carlyle and anticipates both Brown and Thoreau himself, as posthumously remembered. Because a hero can only be recognized prophetically, among either ruins or unbuilt castles, a journey west is primarily psychic. Moving into the future means stepping away from the panoramic. The heroic was there in that panorama, but you did not possess the psychic distance to perceive it. Like Hector and Achilles, the hero must die to be truly heroic.

The west that Thoreau seeks is the resting place of the sun, not the gold fields of California. He associates this psychic west with nature: "The West of which I speak is but another name for the Wild."[34] It is inherently related to dying. "The greater part will be meadow and forest, not only serving for immediate use but preparing a mould against a distant future, by the annual decay of the vegetation which is supports."[35] But in the dying meadows and forests where he walks, there are always echoes of a heroic past, which he conflates with a future that can only exist in death. Thoreau mentions that tree bark was once hawked in the village as medicine and tells us that those old first-growth trees are all gone. Then he moves into an extraordinary image of dying: "The skin of the eland as well as that of other antelope just killed, emits the most delicious perfume of trees and grass. I would have every man so like a wild antelope, so much a part and parcel of Nature, that his very person should thus sweetly advertise our sense of his presence."[36] He seems to be implying that humans, like the antelope, must die in order to emit their true sweetness.

In "Walking," Thoreau explains that a person's name "does not adhere to him when asleep or in anger, or aroused by any passion or inspiration. I seem to hear pronounced by some of his kin at that time his original wild name in some jaw-breaking or else melodious tongue."[37] Here, he seems to prefigure the "family" he discovers in the middle of Spaulding's wood lot:

> I was impressed as if some ancient and altogether admirable and shining family had settled there . . . They seemed to recline on sunbeams . . . [and] nothing can equal the serenity of their lives . . . There was no noise of labor . . . yet I did detect, when the wind lulled and hearing was done away with, the finest imaginable musical hum . . . which perchance was the sound of their thinking.[38]

In this family, Thoreau shows us ourselves in our own golden age. When he thinks of them, he hears their thoughts; the passage implies a timeless, bodiless union of souls. Thus, just as each person can have a sweetness under the skin that only dying can release, he or she has a secret, primitive heritage rediscovered only by dying.

Thoreau follows this insight with another psychic journey, this time to the top of a tall white pine, where he finds, "on the topmost branches only, a few minute and delicate cone-like blossoms, the fertile flower of the white pine looking heavenward."[39] The passage's placement immediately after the extended image of the mystical family on Spaulding's farm is significant. The writer is playing with the idea of both generation and generations, the notion of continuance burgeoning outside of time. His conflation of generation and dying leads him to his conclusion, in which he brings together morning and sunset, spring and autumn, dying and rebirth.

Thoreau has the wonderful ability to let his readers fill in the logistical blanks of his narrative even as he emphasizes his deeper meanings. For instance, when he tells us that he almost always walks westward, he never mentions that he must walk eastward on his return. Instead, he is always heading west, seeming, in each walk, to be circumnavigating the globe. This implied circularity helps to explain his deliberately unclear geography and the fact that he sees a "new prospect" every afternoon when he pays his psychic debt and points himself west.[40] He conveys this sense of circularity when he says, "Above all, we cannot afford to not live in the present."[41] He disdains the past and future as they occur in clock time but points instead at eternal time, which he shares with the pine blossoms and the mystical family, who exist in all time.

From here Thoreau returns to his frequent image of the crowing cockerel. As always, he associates this bird with spring and morning: "It is an expression of the health and soundness of Nature, a brag for all the world—healthiness as of a spring burst forth, a new fountain of the Muses to celebrate this last instant of time."[42] This exact instant is Thoreau's frozen moment outside of time. Punning on his morning imagery, he then tells us he hears the cockerel in "the house of mourning," setting up his reader for the vision that concludes the essay: a realization of sameness in opposites. The writer moves from morning and spring to "We had a remarkable sunset one day last November."[43] At the end of a "cold, gray day" he sees, "the softest brightest morning sunlight . . . while our shadows stretched long over the meadow eastward."[44] The shadows—the heroic shades—return to where they have started. Going west to go east, dying and rebirth, "was not a solitary phenomenon, never to happen again, but it would happen forever and ever an infinite number of evenings."[45] West and the sunset are traditional symbols of the end of life, but in an encircling vision of time, the hero's progress is through dying and out of time. Dying is the ultimate transforming experience, absorbing the walker into the landscape and the hero into his proper sphere in a past outside of time. "The west side of every wood and rising ground gleamed like the boundary of Elysium, and the sun at our backs [indicating an eastward progression] seemed like a gentle herdsman driving us home at evening."[46] "Home" is a psychic space that encompasses living and dying, Concord and Elysium.

III

Both "Wild Apples" and "Huckleberries" are examples of pure Thoreauvian correspondence: the fruits fade out of existence and are commodified; they are rejected by Thoreau's culture, which will suffer for their loss. Perhaps they are the writer's projection of the world's loss of him. "But I now, alas, speak rather from memory than from any recent experience, such ravages have been made."[47]

"Wild Apples" is particularly resonant in the context of his biography. In the essay he discusses three kinds of apple trees: cultivated orchard trees, feral trees, and the indigenous crabapple. He identifies himself most with the feral trees: "*Our* wild apple is only wild like myself, perchance who belong not to the aboriginal race here, but have strayed into the woods from cultivated stock."[48] His relationship with the crabapple seems to parallel the inadequacy he felt about his limited connection to the Native Americans. Just before his death, while putting together the final manuscript copy of this essay, he had set aside his deeply researched notebooks about the native peoples. His most intimate native acquaintance had been Joe Polis, his Penobscot guide on his last trip to Maine. According to Emerson, Thoreau's esteem for Polis equaled his esteem for John Brown, though I suspect that their relationship may not have entirely satisfied Thoreau.[49] Polis taught him a large vocabulary of Penobscot words and had an almost supernatural sense of direction. Yet he also complained about working on Sundays, wanted breakfast before setting out to look for Thoreau's lost companion, got sick, had an insatiable sweet tooth, left matches out in the rain, and lost a foot race to Thoreau.[50] What was admirable in Polis (and Thoreau certainly admired him) as the last hero of a dying race was outside Thoreau's realm of experience. There is direct correlation among the ambivalence of his relationship with Polis, his uncompleted work about the Native Americans, and his search for crabapple blossoms.

When Thoreau was dying, doctors urged him to travel to a warmer, drier climate. Friends suggested southern Europe, Florida, or the West Indies, but he chose Minnesota, which would be cheaper and where he could botanize and gather information for his still-active Native American research. On June 12, 1861, with seventeen-year-old Horace Mann, Jr., as a companion, he traveled by steamboat from Minneapolis to the Lower Sioux Agency to watch a delegation of Dakota receive their federal payment. His biographer Walter Harding writes, "At the request of Governor Ramsey, the half-naked Indians performed a ceremonial dance . . . Thoreau. . . . satisfied himself with purchasing three Indian garments of buckskin and a pair of snowshoes." Thoreau also noted that a flock of gamblers was also aboard the steamboat, and he was sure the natives would soon lose their money.[51]

The historian Corinne Hosfield Smith notes that, before his journey west, "Thoreau's personal interactions with the Native Americans were limited. He met some individuals back home in eastern Massachusetts . . . One of his guides in Maine was Joe Polis, a Penobscot. But these encounters were rare, and generally with select members of the tribes."[52] The scholar John J. Kucich has also discussed the limitations of Thoreau's native encounters: "Thoreau's confrontations with the Penobscot world were like most encounters across this cultural frontier, marked by moments of sudden insight and profound misunderstandings; they were in a word, disorientating, and if they didn't spark the kind of political advocacy that marked his anti-slavery writing, they did help to unsettle his notions of 'the Indian' and America itself."[53]

According to Smith, Thoreau's understanding of the Indians altered after he encountered the Dakotas at the Lower Sioux Agency, though he wrote little about the experience. The payment they had come to receive arrived more than a week late. In the meantime, they had to listen to the ceremonial speeches of the white worthies, including Governor Ramsey, who said he wanted to care for the tribespeople "like a father would his children."[54] After listening to the response of one of the Dakota chiefs, Red Owl, "Thoreau . . . wrote that he 'had the advantage [over the white men] in point of truth and earnestness, and therefore eloquence.'" Thoreau was also impressed by Chief Little Crow, and he was gratified to see "one of the Indians start a fire for his pipe by striking a flint and using the spark to ignite maple wood fragments. Finally [Thoreau] was getting a chance to see for himself the techniques and habits of native culture that he had only read about."[55]

Thoreau recorded his impressions of the Dakota dancing, choosing to write in the present tense as if he were freezing the moment in time: "12 musicians on drums & others strike arrows against bows. The dancers blow some flutes—keep good time—move feet & shoulders, one or both—no shirts—5 bands there."[56] Another member of the steamboat excursion also recorded the occasion, displaying a far different reaction: "On the whole . . . it was . . . a pitiable disgusting spectacle . . . If there is any sincere interest . . . in elevating the moral and social condition of these poor, childish creatures, all such relics of barbarism as these dances should be discouraged."[57] Clearly, when compared to his fellow travelers, Thoreau was not scandalized by what he saw.

The tourists purchased small souvenirs from the Dakota. Smith writes:

> Thoreau carried away . . . three pieces of Dakota buckskin. He now owned a dress, a shirt jacket, and a pair of trousers. His fascination with the Indians had obviously led him somehow to acquire these items . . . Was Thoreau acting out of concern, hoping to financially assist at least one of the Dakota? . . . Or was he merely thinking of preserving evidence of this Native American culture before it was extinguished?[58]

After the steamboat returned to Minneapolis, Thoreau and Mann began their journey home instead of continuing into the second half of their planned trip. Perhaps the encounter with the Dakotas was a satisfying climax to the journey, or perhaps he was so discouraged by what he saw that he yearned to be back in his familiar environs. In her book, Smith explains that, soon after Thoreau's visit, a war broke out between the Dakotas and the U.S. government, and the bands Thoreau had seen were decimated. She speculates that if Thoreau had lived, he would have written about their annihilation.

According to Thoreau's biographer, Robert D. Richardson, Jr., "the trip was a tragic failure in most respects."[59] As a hero's crusade, however, it was an extraordinary success, for during his journey Thoreau identified his symbolic connection with the Native Americans. In "Wild Apples," he writes,

> I never saw the Crab-Apple until May, 1861 . . . It was a half fabulous flower to me . . . On entering Michigan I began to notice from the cars a tree with handsome, rose-colored flowers . . . On entering St. Anthony's Falls, I was sorry to be told I was too far north for the Crab-Apple. Nevertheless I succeeded in finding it about eight miles west of the Falls; touched it and smelled it, and secured a lingering corymb of flowers for my herbarium.[60]

When he finds this fleeting and "half fabulous" flower, the hero-as-naturalist vindicates his life. The dying man, holding the withered flower, can go home with physical proof of a life lived deliberately.[61]

Although he celebrates the crabapple in a later section of "Wild Apples," he chooses to open the essay with a discussion of the cultivated orchard. "It is remarkable how closely the history of the Apple-tree is connected with that of man . . . Indeed in this sense it is the most civilized of all trees."[62] Yet most people, he believes, are not capable of experiencing apples properly: "I see the stream of their evanescent and celestial qualities going to heaven from [the farmer's] cart, while the pulp and skin and core only go to market."[63] He offers several classical allusions to apples and points out that, for the Greeks, the word *apple* signified all fruit. In his eyes, something as beautiful as an apple has more meaning as an idea than as a commodity.

In both "Wild Apples" and "Huckleberries," Thoreau invokes, as always, the sense of being ready, finally, to perceive what has always been in one's world. By removing ourselves from the social and economic contingencies of an apple or a handful of berries and eating it with our full attention, we can experience the fruit completely. We can taste sweet and sour and, behind them, leaves, twigs, bark, and soil. We can discover the essence of plant and earth, rain, and finally, as the sugar reasserts itself, the flavor of sunlight. As he does in "Walking," Thoreau presents the possibility that we are living in a golden age but cannot perceive it. Consequently, the divine is passing away; "for nectar and ambrosia are only those fine flavors of every earthly fruit which our coarse palates fail to perceive, . . . just as we occupy the heaven of the gods without knowing it."[64] More urgently, he insists that this dissolution of the divine is happening as he speaks, and he reinforces this anxiety by closing the essay with a quotation from the book of Joel: "The vine is dried up, and the fig-tree languisheth; the pomegranate-tree, the palm-leaf also, and the apple-tree, even all the trees of the field, are withered: because joy has withered away from the sons of men."[65] According to the scholar Ronald Wesley Hoag, Thoreau is telling us that, "like the old world apple-tree that soon ran wild in the new world, Americans must learn what true nature is and align themselves with it. To do so is to restore or repossess Eden, while the alternative is described in the essay's *or else* conclusion."[66] In my view, this warning is primarily a reminder to look now, for this will all soon be gone. "Wild Apples" is an elegy for both the apple trees and the man who is sharing his perceptions of them.

"Wild Apples" also offers an interesting insight into why the transcendentalists, despite their progressive opinions, avoided organized reform movements. Thoreau disapproved of alcoholic beverages, yet in this essay he rails against the temperance movement's role in the demise of the wild apple: "The era of the Wild Apple will soon be past. It is a fruit that will probably become extinct in New England."[67] He describes an enormous wild apple orchard in a neighboring town, which the owner had cut down to prevent the apples from being made into cider. To Thoreau, this carnage is an example of society turning against itself. Divorced from nature, society can no longer see the value of its beautiful creation and kills it without recognizing the loss. Yet in another sense, dying asserts itself as a truly transcendental experience. Apples, like the antelope he describes in "Walking," must die to emit their greatest sweetness: "For I know that they lie concealed, fallen into hollows long since covered up by leaves of the tree itself—a proper kind of packing."[68] He is ridiculing the terminology of commerce but also punning on burial and reinforcing our sense of the utter sweetness of spirit.

As he celebrates what is soon to die, Thoreau adapts the New Testament story of Jesus and the sacrament. In the Bible, only the original disciples take the sacrament from Jesus, who asks his disciples to eat and drink "in memory of me."[69] Thoreau does the same in "Wild Apples," sharing the sacrament with an unnamed companion—perhaps simply the reader. Switching from past tense to present, he writes, "Now we both greedily fill our pockets with them—bending to drink the juice—and grow more social with the wine."[70] As we read these words, we take communion with the apple and with the writer, who knows he will be dead by the time we read them.

All creation partakes of this sacrament; "not only the Indian, but many indigenous insects, birds, and quadrupeds, welcomed the apple tree to these shores." Thoreau lists the birds that nest there—bluebirds, robins, cedar waxwings (he calls them cherry birds), downy woodpeckers, kingbirds, partridges, and owls "warbled in its boughs and so became orchard birds."[71] For Thoreau, sustenance always exists on several levels; and these wild creatures, by choosing to partially domesticate themselves in the orchard, become his avatars. The animals are partaking of both the apple's demise and his own when they burrow and feed in the tree, taking leave of the dying even as they accustom themselves to their new existence. Wildness inheres in the apple orchard; otherwise, it would not have been able to exist in its own wild state.

Throughout Thoreau's writing, we see his fascination with domestic animals' potential to become feral—from the bay horse, the hound dog, and the turtledove in *Walden* to the neighbor's cow that jumps the fence and swims in the river like a buffalo.[72]

In "Wild Apples," he comically describes cows browsing on young trees, transforming them into spreading, thorny bushes "until at last [the trees] are so broad they become their own fence, when some interior shoot . . . darts upward for joy; it has not forgotten its high calling, and bears its own peculiar fruit in triumph."[73] No longer a threat, the cows rest in the trees' shade, eat the fruit, and spread the seed.

The anecdote also functions an allegorical autobiography. The cows are village culture, which "held down" Thoreau until his "interior shoot" was able to "dart upward for joy" and "bear its own peculiar fruit"—for example, the very essay we are reading. The cows may once have been foes, but they have become readers who enjoy his shade and taste his fruit. The spreading bottom, which has served its purpose, is the writer's body. Now his essence survives in a joyous striving into the light as pure spirit. After his readers taste his fruit, they can choose to spread his seed.

"Huckleberries" expresses many of these same ideas but it is different in tone. Because Thoreau died before he could edit it for publication, it retains the language of the lecture and addresses the reader-listener with great immediacy: "I presume everyone in my audience knows what a huckleberry is—has seen a huckleberry—gathered a huckleberry—nay, tasted a huckleberry."[74] This statement embodies the tragic irony of the lecture, for he is addressing the last generation to experience the free profusion of huckleberries.[75] The tension, a familiar one for Thoreau, lies in the ephemeral, spiritual condition of nature and her lovers and her consequent vulnerability to an avaricious culture. "The black ones shine with such a gloss—every one its eye on you, and the blue are so large and firm, that you can hardly believe them to be huckleberries at all, or edible, but you seem to have travelled to a foreign country, or else are dreaming."[76] He describe the berries as "strong" and "moist," constructing a nearly erotic image that pulls together the dichotomous forces that create the berries' world. As "eyes," the berries are witness to the harvesters' intentions. It is hard to believe they are edible because something possessed of such a divine nature should not merely exist to fill the belly. The world Thoreau has created for his huckleberry field is curiously divorced from time and place, despite the fact that the preceding paragraphs have listed the varieties' precise ripening dates. These are pure huckleberries of the mind. The woods may be full of berries in July and August, but only the discerning eye can locate the dreamscape of their truest existence. Even so, he ominously undercuts this splendid vision when he notes, "They are a firmer berry than most of the whortleberry family—and hence are the most marketable."[77]

Native Americans are also invoked in the essay. In Thoreau's view, the native peoples took their identity from wild nature, as the ancient epic heroes did. He speculates on links between his own observations and native traditions. For instance, after describing dried huckleberries on an autumn bush, he suggests that seeing them in that natural form may have inspired the Native Americans to dry them over fires. He also notes that, like the native peoples (and unlike the wild apple), the huckleberry is a truly indigenous American fruit: "The ancient Greeks and Romans appear not to have made much account of strawberries, huckleberries, melons, etc. because they had not got them."[78]

As I mentioned in chapter 2, Thoreau had long been playing on the old expression of "going a-blackberrying"—that is, going to the devil—when writing about going huckleberrying. In *Walden*, he suggests that if John Field and his family give up their desire for meat and coffee, they can all pick huckleberries together in the summer.[79] In "Civil Disobedience," after he is thrown out of jail in the morning, he joins a group of women and children who are going huckleberrying.[80] In both cases, he talks about going huckleberrying in the same tone of triumph and self-mockery that he uses to express his determination to "know beans" in *Walden*.[81] He is thumbing his nose at society's expectations of him. In the essay "Huckleberries," the image works at the same level, but its scope is widened. Thoreau begins with a discussion about what society considers "little things" and "great things."[82] To leave the world of great things to go huckleberrying seems to imply a deliberate shirking of responsibility or an immaturity of character—literally, going to the devil. But Thoreau proceeds to turn this interpretation inside out. If what the world thinks of as little things are great things and vice versa, then what seems to be a perversion of character is following one's own genius rather than following the devil. In other words, leaving behind the great things of the world is in fact leaving them to the devil.

Thoreau's views are clarified when he talks about Captain Church's raid during King Philip's War, which appears after a long summary of European observations of Native Americans' treatment of huckleberries. He argues that white chroniclers disprove their own belief that Indian savagery was apparent in their food; they themselves have described the Indians preparing elaborate dishes from indigenous foods without any knowledge of European cookery. Then he tells us about an incident in which "Captain Church . . . came across a large body of Indians, chiefly squaws, gathering whortleberries . . . and killed and took prisoner sixty-six of them—some throwing away their baskets in their flight."[83] Women picking berries is a little thing; men making war is a great thing. (When describing his own huckleberrying, Thoreau makes the point that women and children are his usual companions.) In the face of the ferocious attack, the women must necessarily disrupt their peaceful tasks. The writer gives a matter-of-fact and unemotional account of the carnage, letting his audience decide if the devil lives in little things or great things, and then goes on to give more accounts of Indian puddings made with wild berries.

As in "Wild Apples," the elegiac in "Huckleberries" encompasses the fruit, the Native Americans, and himself: "The last Indian of Nantucket, who died a few years ago, was very properly represented in a painting . . . with a basketful of huckleberries in his hand . . . I trust that I may not outlive the last of the huckleberries."[84] Moreover, the essay is more directly autobiographical than "Wild Apples" is. Thoreau talks about his own childhood and childhood generally. He shows us how his own sensibilities have grown from his childhood experiences, suggesting the fluidity of child and adult consciousness in relation to nature. "I have served my apprenticeship and have since done considerable journeywork in the huckleberry field," he puns.[85] He uses the familiar theme of food taken as sacrament, stating that huckleberries " seemed offered to us not so much for food as for sociality, inviting us to pic-nic with Nature. We pluck and eat them in remembrance of her. It is a sort of sacrament—a communion—the *not* forbidden fruits which no serpent tempts us to eat."[86]

Thoreau's "us" however, must be defined, because he does show us the serpent in the garden. The vulnerability of nature is identical to the vulnerability of childlike consciousness. Always with Thoreau, we see what we are willing to see. "Us" is the group of initiates who refuse to give entrance to the serpent, but the serpent comes nonetheless. Purity is the family that has put aside worldliness and gone huckleberrying, but worldliness also comes to the fields in the guise of a family. "I once met a whole family, father, mother, and children, ravaging a huckleberry field in this wise: They cut up the bushes as they went and beat them over the edge of a bushel basket, till they had it full of berries, ripe and green, leaves, sticks, etc., and so they passed along out of my sight like wild men."[87] This is the scene of carnage he doesn't describe when he talks about Captain Church in the huckleberry patch. The white family and the soldiers, not the Indian women, are savages. He makes us reconsider the idea of childhood among the huckleberries, to recognize that some of the "children" have known the serpent all along. Revisiting his childhood, he widens the picture to include not just the solitary boy on the hillside but a mass of marauding boys: "There was a Young America then, which has become Old America, but its principles and motives are still the same . . . Every boy rushed to the hill and hastily selected a spot—shouted, 'I speak for this place' . . . and this was sometimes considered good law for the huckleberry field. At any rate, it is a law similar to this by which we have taken possession of the territory of the Indians and Mexicans."[88]

At this point in the essay, Thoreau offers an ironic and poignant view of the incipient huckleberry industry. The fields are rented out in lots and can only be plucked for profit now. Instead of being peddled door to door by children, the berries are sold from the butcher's cart. The butcher calls to mind Captain Church's raid and the rapacious family. Getting huckleberries goes from an act of innocence to a synonym for violence and carnage: "You all know what it is to go a-beefsteaking. It is to knock your old fellow laborer Bright on the head."[89] Of course he is speaking of his compassion for domestic animals, but at a deeper level "fellow laborer" resonates with the violence that humans perform on one another. The phrase reminds us of the Indian women harvesting berries and perhaps, further south, other laborers in other fields.

IV

Perhaps the most beautiful and elegiac of the late essays is "Autumnal Tints." What the other essays suggest this one fully delineates: that dying can be the most fully realized transcendental experience. Again, Thoreau starts with the Native Americans, who had mostly vanished from the Concord area long before his birth. Thoreau spent his whole life searching for traces of them, repopulating his homeland in his imagination. In his mind, the autumn colors evoke a vanished race of heroes, whose perfection in memory is reflected by the yearly glory of dying in nature, a reenactment of the instant moment of the native people's disappearance.

Considering the purple "Indian grass," Thoreau says, "The expression of this grass haunted me for a week, like the glance of an eye. It stands like an Indian chief taking a last look at his favorite hunting-grounds."[90] His description adds to the stock tradition of the last, lone Indian, whose frozen moment of parting is in keeping with nineteenth-century deathbed vigils. As Thoreau will in the moment of his own dying, the chief at this instant looks back rather than ahead, living completely in the moment of perfect separation. Autumn comes as a half-known memory of the golden age: "[The grasses] take you by surprise . . . thus early in the season, as if they were a gay encampment of red men, or other foresters, of whose arrival you had not heard."[91] Much like the mystical family in "Walking," these foresters exist outside of time.

In "Thoreau's Multiple Modernities," the scholar William Rossi argues that "a deeper reason for inattention [to nature] stems from the fragmentation not only of modern awareness, but of memory."

> This is the second feature of modernity [that "Autumnal Tints"] counters, describ[ing] a condition in which the depth of being has been forgotten and, with it, the depth and multi-dimensional temporalities of lived experience. Here it is important to note, that Thoreau frames the essay as an exercise in remembering as well as representing the fall, "a phenomenon that is scarcely remembered from year to year" even by the majority who have witnessed it . . . If, as the narrator claims, "by the twentieth of August, everywhere in the woods and swamps we are reminded of the fall," then we—author, narrator, and audience—are not so much learning something new as being awakened to what at some level we have always known: our own mortality . . . Yet far from expressing melancholy or loss, the narrator represents such awareness as attainment of full maturity.[92]

"Autumnal Tints" is full of martial imagery. Of the red maple, Thoreau writes, "I am thrilled by . . . it, bearing aloft its scarlet standard for the regiment of green-clad foresters." He tells us that "some trees, as small hickories, appear to have dropped their leaves simultaneously, as a soldier grounds arms at a signal." In the voice of the scarlet oak, he says, "I bring up the rear in my red coat. We scarlet ones, alone of the Oaks, have not given up the fight."[93] It is important, however, not to interpret this imagery in relation to the Civil War underway at the time of his final revision; he makes it clear that Union's tawdry patriotism is not his concern. Rather, he is talking about the classical ideal of heroism that exists outside of time. His full-leafed heroes, like his conception of John Brown, are immortal and infinitely superior to the moment. "Shall that dirty roll of bunting in the gun-house be all the colors a village can display?"[94]

Autumn pauses only in the writer's imagination, and its temporality is relevant to the frozen instant of dying. Significantly, the scarlet oaks are fighting a battle in a war already lost. Thoreau is concerned with the transitional moment between life and death. For example, he is fascinated by the afterimage of trees on the ground just after all the leaves have fallen, describing this phenomenon several times: "I would rather say that I first observe the tree thus flat on the ground like a permanent colored shadow, and they suggest to look for the boughs that bore them."[95] The colored shadow, like any shadow, is impermanent except in memory; an afternoon breeze will quickly disperse it. Rather, the leaves on the ground encourage one to look at the now denuded boughs, another act of imaginative memory.

Thoreau's essay juxtaposes the joyous and the somber. "So [the leaves] troop to their last resting place, light and frisky . . . Merrily they go scampering over the earth."[96] The writer notes that birds' nests, perennial symbols of spring and new life, are now filling with withered leaves. To accept as one's fate an instant of glorious color, then quickly wither away to shadow and memory, is the heroic embracing of dying, the same death that Achilles chooses in the *Iliad*. As Homer writes, "What good's to be won from tears that chill the spirit? / So the immortals spun our lives."[97]

In the "Sugar-Maple" section of the essay, Thoreau writes: "[The maples] are worth more than they have cost—though one selectman, while setting them out, took the cold which occasioned his death."[98] Though he usually disparages the village selectmen, here he shows us one willingly and beautifully giving his life for a principle. Setting out young trees is the equivalent of burying seeds in the ground for the future, and the selectman has given his life in this service.[99]

In the "Fallen Leaves" section, Thoreau explicitly inverts Virgil's (and later Dante's) simile of the souls gathering on the shores of Acheron. In the *Aeneid*, Virgil writes, "As many souls / As leaves that yield their hold on boughs and fall / Through forests in the early frosts of autumn."[100] In contrast, Thoreau writes, "I reach a quiet cove, where I unexpectedly find myself surrounded by myriads of leaves, like fellow voyagers."[101] He even refers to himself as Charon, the mythological ferryman to the underworld. The inversion implies a fluidity between myth and reality, the shadowy past and the present reality. The opportunity to sacrifice one's life beautifully and meaningfully always has and always will exist. "[The leaves] that have flown so loftily, how contentedly do they return to the dust again, and are laid low, resigned to lie and decay at the foot of a tree, and afford nourishment to new generations of their kind, as well as to flutter on high! They teach us how to die."[102]

The final section of the essay, "The Scarlet Oak," is among Thoreau's most ecstatic examples of nature writing. Again, he communicates his transcendental vision of the old Puritan idea of translation, that fluid instant in which the body gives way to the spirit, this time in an astonishingly close reading of the leaves themselves: "They have so little *terra firma* that they appear melting away in the light and scarcely obstruct our view" of the sky and the light.[103] Like the long shoots of the wild apple, the leaves aspire to the light; they even become part of the light, stopped in the instant of transition from one state to another: "Lifted higher and higher, and sublimated more and more, putting off some earthiness and cultivating more intimacy with the light, they have at length the least amount of earthy matter, and the greatest spread and grasp of skyey influences. There they dance, arm in arm with the light."[104] The poignancy of the scarlet oaks lies in the fact that they are the last leaves to change color, and they reflect the whole history of autumn in their experience of it. And, as always with Thoreau, only the mind prepared to see may create the eye with which to see. He notes that many people see only gray in November, even though the end of autumn is when the brightest colors appear. Yet these brilliant backlit reds are suffused with shadow, so one can truly see them only from a distance. The function of memory is to stand back and see holistically, which is not possible when one is deep inside the actual experience. The act of dying gives the final, passionate surge to the leaves' last days; and as slim and aerial as their physical state is, it is the idea of them that makes the greater impression: "The very rails reflect a rosy light at this hour and season. You see a redder tree than exists."[105]

Although the essay has nothing to do with war, Thoreau uses martial imagery throughout, even ending with a hunting simile. He has prepared us for this ending by his repeated reference to the evergreens as foresters. The tragic beauty of the dying leaves can exist only amid the perennial greens of the pines. What the hunter "kills," however, is not a bird but what Thoreau refers to in "Walking" as "our winged thoughts."[106] The good hunter may sight the idea of autumn, that frozen but perpetual moment of transition, if he or she has a strong enough desire to experience it. "The Scarlet Oak must, in a sense, be in your eye when you go forth. We cannot see anything until we are possessed with the idea of it, take it into our heads—and then we can hardly see anything else."[107] The instantaneous and the rare are constantly before us, but we cannot experience them until we have traveled the right psychic distance. Thoreau writes, "These bright leaves which I have mentioned are not the exception, but the rule; for I believe that all leaves, even grasses and mosses, acquire brighter colors before their fall. When you come to observe faithfully the changes of each humblest plant, you find that each has, sooner or later, its peculiar autumnal tint."[108] After reading this passage, I find it impossible to believe that Thoreau forgot his rarefied idea of John Brown when he returned to nature writing. Instead, like the oak leaves, he "sublimated" the idea, "putting off some earthiness and cultivating more intimacy with the light."[109] In his vision, Brown, like the autumn leaves, is forever frozen in the instant between living and dying, thereby teaching us how to die.

V

Maturity is one of the great themes in Thoreau, and its equivalent in nature is ripeness. *A Week on the Concord and Merrimack Rivers* ends on the cusp of the transition from summer to autumn, with the imminent separation of the brothers dividing the spirit from the body. In the *Walden* chapter "Higher Laws," Thoreau tells us that it is natural for boys to go into the woods with guns; but if they want to really become men, they must put aside their guns and hunt ideas instead. From his early career to his late, Thoreau moved meanderingly from spring to autumn, morning to evening. The four essays I've discussed in this chapter treat late summer and autumn with a Keatsian sensuality, as though all of nature and all of humanity's possibilities husband themselves for a final and infinite moment of perfect dying. Though this movement toward perfection is everywhere in nature if one is willing to experience it, in a human its existence is as miraculous as the colors of autumn would be if they occurred only once in centuries. This idea of the heroic exemplified in a truly natural man is ultimately how Thoreau viewed John Brown. Brown became his heroic logos: no longer an individual, or even human, he now became the language of nature.

Why did Thoreau choose Brown as his representative of absolute heroism in dying? Beyond the obvious biographical similarities (for instance, both were New England surveyors with a distaste for fancy dinners), we can sense that both were extraordinary yet ordinary, men who knew the proper time to die and therefore lived by nature's designs. For Thoreau, Brown represented an idea (as he tells us several times in "A Plea for Captain John Brown"), which is why the actual politics behind the actions at Harpers Ferry ultimately didn't matter to him. This idea was not new to Thoreau's thinking, but he chose Brown as the one human representative of the magnificent order of creation. In the gaunt old man from Connecticut he saw not the vigilante but the scarlet oak. In his eyes, the greatest good a man can do is to die for a principle, the equivalent of dying at the proper moment of ripeness.

This is not to say that Thoreau was indifferent to antislavery activism. On the contrary, he believed that slavery was the nation's great moral failure, and he had long been impatient with the pusillanimity of northern abolitionists. As the scholar Philip Cafaro notes, "in defending Brown, Thoreau reiterates points made in his earliest anti-slavery pieces. Illegal acts are justified in opposing slavery. What is new is his treatment of heroism: the rare irruption of virtue in the political realm . . . By dying for their principles, Brown and his men give concrete proof that each of us may sacrifice for higher ideals."[110] In other words, like nature, heroism should be a process; the example of Brown and his men should be like good seeds planted in the earth.

In "Autumnal Tints" Thoreau tells us, "For aught we know, as strange a man as any of these is always at our elbow."[111] This statement resonates with another in "A Plea for Captain John Brown": "But let some significant event like the present occur in our midst, and we discover, often, this distance and strangeness between us and our nearest neighbor."[112] A sense of the uncanny pervades both essays. In "Autumnal Tints," Thoreau imagines a group of absolutely dissimilar men studying the same autumn prospect: for instance, he pictures a selectman (not the one who set out the maples) who is thinking of property values and boundaries. Working from the premise that "a man sees what concerns him," Thoreau leaves us to imagine how his three other hypothetical gazers—the theologian Emanuel Swedenborg, a "Feegee-Islander," and Julius Caesar—see themselves reflected in what they view.[113] Presumably, Swedenborg sees the mystical, the islander sees the wild, and Caesar sees the heroic, thereby representing a symbiosis of Thoreau's vision of nature and himself. The strangeness lies in the fact that no person can completely comprehend the vision of another person or how he sees himself in relation to nature.

The strangeness in "A Plea for Captain John Brown" expands this notion into a consideration of our ignorance about our neighbors. We may chide and castigate them all our lives, but they may still surprise us by seeing something entirely different from what we see. Thoreau writes, "It is the difference of constitution, of intelligence, and faith, not streams and mountains, that make impassable boundaries between individuals and between states. None but the like-minded can come plenipotentiary to our court."[114] With "our court," he evokes not the military court at Harpers Ferry but the vision of the like-minded. He sees both Brown and the landscape as a compendium of the mystical, the wild, and the heroic. Yet, to his fury, his neighbors see only a lunatic, just as they see only a crank in Henry Thoreau and money in the landscape.

Throughout "A Plea for Captain John Brown," Thoreau refers to the abolitionist in the past tense, even though he was still alive when he first delivered the lecture from which the essay arose. Moreover, in none of the three related essays does Thoreau describe the hanging, though he certainly knew that Brown had shown great courage on the gallows. This choice of omission recalls another of the ancient Greek authors whom he held dear: the playwright Aeschylus. In *Agamemnon*, the first of three tragedies in a cycle known as the *Oresteia*, the chorus describes in graphic detail the events leading up to the death of Iphigenia but never describes the actual sacrifice. We see her hoisted onto the altar, and there the chorus stops. So in a sense, the act is never completed; the girl, forever suspended at the moment of sacrifice, is also suspended over the entire trilogy. Thoreau borrows this technique for his Brown trilogy. In the essays, Brown is everywhere and nowhere, neither alive nor dead but always in the moment of translation—immortal. "This morning, perchance, Captain Brown was hung . . . He is not Old Brown anymore; he is an Angel of Light."[115] It is the same light that shines down on both the scarlet oak and the wild apple, the same light that bathes a hillside on a November afternoon.

In "A Plea for Captain John Brown," Thoreau says, "I am here to plead his cause with you. I plead not for his life but for his character—his immortal life."[116] Brown's immortal life, like the immortal life of nature, is the significant organizing principle in all three essays. As Reynolds notes, "perhaps 'the living North' appreciated Brown, but Thoreau knew well that not all the North was living, in his sense of the word."[117] Of Brown's raid, Thoreau writes, "This event advertises [to] me that there is such a thing as death—the possibility of a man's dying. It seems as if no man had ever died in America before, for in order to die, you must have lived." Like the autumn leaves, Brown and his men, "in teaching us how to die, have at the same time taught us how to live."[118] During the process of dying, Brown is the great human exemplar of life in nature.

In the essay "Martyrdom," Thoreau addresses him: "You, Agricola, are fortunate, not only because your life was glorious, but because your death was timely."[119] Yet in "The Last Days of John Brown," based on speech he composed six months after Brown's death, Thoreau has come to believe that Brown never died at all. He says of himself that he "commonly attend[s] more to Nature than to man, but any affecting human event may blind our eyes to natural objects." Yet he goes on to write that when he sees a familiar bird "still diving quietly in the river . . . it suggest[s] that this bird might continue to dive here when Concord is no more."[120] Thoreau is pointing directly to eternity: just as nature shall outlive the petty world of Concord, so Brown's immortal heroism will outlive the disreputable time of American chattel slavery. He concludes the essay by saying, "I meet him at every turn. He is more alive than he ever was. He has earned his immortality."[121]

Immortality is the great characteristic that Brown shares with nature. Always Thoreau emphasizes their closeness. In both "A Plea for Captain John Brown" and his Journal, he mentions the close relations that Brown formed with the Native Americans. On December 3, 1859, he writes, "When I heard of John Brown and his wife weeping at length, it was as if the rocks sweated." Thoreau is acutely aware that Brown is dying as the year is dying. On November 15 he writes about the plentiful seeds of the white pine and shagbarks, which "still hung on the trees, though most had fallen." He makes this observation in the middle of his complaint that Massachusetts is "not taking any steps for the defense of her citizens who are likely to be carried to Virginia as witnesses, and exposed to the violence of a slaveholding mob." On November 28, in his greatest rush of words about Brown's heroism in the face of an unheroic and prosaic North, he pauses to say, "This has been a very pleasant month, with quite a few Indian-summer days." The people around Thoreau are reactionaries, and the writer battles daily with impatience and rage; but Brown and nature maintain their serenity, acceptance, faith, and sanity.[122]

At the end of "The Last Days of John Brown," Thoreau writes that Brown "is no longer working in secret. He works in public, and in the clearest light that shines on this land."[123] The paragraph says nothing about Brown's actual death but refers to "the day of his translation."[124] Like the animals and the trees, he has been translated to a higher heaven and has earned his immortality.

VI

If Thoreau had lived through the Civil War, what would he have thought about Emancipation, the uptick in Union aggressions and victories, and the fact that so many Union men fought and died courageously for a principle? Would he have felt that the buried seeds of John Brown and his men had borne good fruit? Certainly Emerson believed so. But during Thoreau's final months and the first year of the war, he remained skeptical. He wrote nothing in his Journal about the war, mentioning it only in a letter to his friend Franklin Sanborn, written from Minnesota. "I am not even so well informed as to the progress of the war as you suppose," he tells Sanborn, saying he'd only seen one eastern paper, the abolitionist *Tribune,* during the past five weeks. "The people of Minnesota have *seemed* to me more cold—to feel less implicated in this war than the people of Massachusetts." Here he exhibits a touch of pride in his home state. He does mention, however, that recently he had heard much weeping when the Union volunteers left the Minnesota town of Redwing, though he ironically notes that there was little weeping when the regulars were sent out to fight the Native Americans. The remainder of his letter describes his visit to the Lower Sioux Agency.[125]

Botany predominated in Thoreau's thoughts during the last year of his life. In a March 12, 1862, response to an admirer named Myron Benton, he declares, "If I were to live, I should have much to report on Natural

History generally."[126] The only mention of Brown appears in March 30, 1862, letter *to* Thoreau written by his New Bedford friend Daniel Ricketson, a member of the Society of Friends: "Two young men in a buggy-wagon have just driven up the road singing in very sonorous strains the 'John Brown' chorus. I wish its pathetic and heart-stirring appeals could reach the inward ears of Congress and the President."[127] At this point Thoreau could no longer answer letters and depended on Sophia to write back to his correspondents. Though she was as committed an abolitionist as the Quaker Ricketson was, her letter makes no mention of Brown or his song.

In my view, however, Thoreau's passionate feelings about Brown and his men did not simply vanish but were translated into his last great natural history passion: seeds. This enthusiasm was not new; a fascination with seeds, both actual and symbolic, is evident in much of his work—for instance, in *Walden.* As I have pointed out, seed imagery permeates the four nature essays I've discussed in this chapter as well as the three Brown essays. But by the end of his life, Thoreau's lifelong fascination with seeds had blossomed into powerful insight and understanding. In fact, much of his writings about seeds and forest trees anticipated Charles Darwin's *On the Origin of Species,* which was published in the United States in 1860.

The essay "The Succession of Forest Trees" was culled from a work that Thoreau didn't live to complete, "The Dispersion of Forest Trees."[128] For many years, scholars did not take Thoreau's science seriously. Thus, as the environmental historian Laura Dassow Walls explains, "the text in which he most fully negotiated the difficult passage between poetry and science [fell] between them into obscurity."[129] This situation has changed in the past few decades. The scientific accuracy of his late work is now generally accepted, and his detailed observations on flowering and leaf-out times, bird arrival dates, and ice-out dates are being used to track climate change in eastern Massachusetts. The scholar Kristen Case writes, "This reassessment of Thoreau's late writings has been central to the emergence of the ecocritical approach to literature in the past two decades."[130] Nonetheless, though "Succession" is currently receiving attention as a work of natural history, it has not till now been grouped with Thoreau's late prophetic essays or linked to his writings about John Brown.

In September 1860, almost a year after Brown's raid on Harpers Ferry, Thoreau presented "Succession" as a lecture to the Middlesex Agricultural Society in a gathering at the Concord Town Hall. He opened by facetiously announcing, "Every man is entitled to come to Cattle-shows," an echo of the mock-humble opening to "A Plea for Captain John Brown": "I trust you will pardon me for being here."[131] In both instances he then moves into prophecy.

In "Succession," the birth of trees is predicated on the dying of forests and animals. Therefore, along with the prophet-naturalist speaker, nature is the hero of the essay. Like the Brown essays, "Succession" has a strong first-person narrator. Walls notes, "Throughout . . . he insists on fore-grounding his own role as agent, both in the field and at the podium."[132] Thoreau begins with images of biblical prophecy such as the walking staff and the ram's horn and says, "Let me lead you back into your wood-lots again."[133] Noting that the farmers in his audience may have fantastic beliefs about why pine woods spring up when hardwoods are cut down and vice versa, he tells them that he has come before them to be their eyes and truth bearer. The most obvious fact, he tells them, is the most remarkable: though slips and cuttings may be used in orchards, in nature all trees come from seeds. The role of the prophet "remains only to show how the seed is transported from where it grows to where it is planted."[134]

Thoreau begins with the pines, explaining that their seed is physically designed so that, "when committed to the wind, . . . it may transport the seed and extend the range of the species."[135] This doesn't just anticipate Darwin, but also shows the heroic qualities of nature. Seeds are nature's avatars and children; they fly off as bravely and cheerfully as the autumn leaves and Brown's men do, most of them to their death. Many will be digested by animals or will fall on infertile ground; others will sprout seed-lings that will be choked out in their first years. He tells the audience that acorns and other nuts, carried by birds and quadrupeds, may also sprout in pine woods. With the right kind of vision, a visitor may see the little oaks among the pines. When the pine forest is cut down—killed—what was obvious only to Thoreau will become apparent to all. This destruction recalls his descriptions in "Huckleberries." When woods are cut down or burned, bushes spring up to feed birds and people. So humankind is made to participate in nature's resurrection.

Only Thoreau, the prophet of nature, can interpret this parable of seeds for his audience. One species takes a risk for the sake of its own kind, while another heroically offers its life for the sake of another species. "We send a party of woodchoppers to cut down the pines, and so rescue an oak forest."[136] Nature's creatures do similar work. "The squirrel was then engaged in accomplishing two objects, to wit, laying up a store of Winter food for itself, and planting a hickory wood for all creation."[137] The squirrel is nature's emissary: its death can propagate an entire forest. This gives the squirrel a semi-divine autonomy so it can accomplish nature's ends. If the squirrel is killed by an animal or human predator, a brave troop of hardwoods will spring up. Here the images in "Succession" are reminiscent of those in "Autumnal Tints" and "A Plea for Captain John Brown." The little hardwoods planted by the martyred squirrels will also die if the pines are not cut down, but "they do better for a few years under their shelter than they would anywhere else."[138] The pines become the oaks' nurses. The pines die after fulfilling their destiny, having given their lives for a new species.

Thoreau speaks of how the British use pine woods as a nursery for young oak trees, "merely adopting the method of Nature, which she long ago made patent to all."[139] Elsewhere he repeats the image, calling nature the "patent office at the seat of government of the universe."[140] He uses the language of agriculture prophetically. "So when we experiment in planting forests, we find ourselves at last doing as Nature does. Would it not be well to consult with Nature at the outset? for she is the most extensive and experienced planter of us all."[141]

Thoreau shares the parable of a squirrel hunter, who found a walnut tree "which bore particularly good nuts, but in going to gather them one Fall, he found that he had been anticipated by a family of a dozen red squirrels." The tree was hollow and the hunter gathered "a bushel and three pecks . . . and they supplied him and his family for the Winter."[142] Human and squirrel become equal as they vie for the same winter store. The man may have come to kill squirrels but instead discovers they have left him a great bounty.

After disproving the notion that acorns and other nuts can lie dormant in pine woods for an indefinite period and still maintain their vitality, Thoreau goes on to show how certain small seeds do lie dormant in the soil for centuries, germinating when they finally have the opportunity. He tells his listeners about what he found when the Hunt House in Concord was taken down. Noticing that the date 1703 was etched into the chimney, he concludes that it was left from the newer part of the house and guesses that the other section could have been up to a half century older. When the cellar was uncovered, several unknown weeds sprouted, as did tobacco, which was once cultivated in the area. "The cellar had been filled up this year, and four of those plants, including the tobacco, are now again extinct in that locality."[143] Nature, using man as her agent, operates in slow time, letting centuries lapse between dying and rebirth, but only her existence makes that rebirth a possibility.

The essay nears its close with the anecdote of the *Poitrine jaune grosse,* the giant yellow squash Thoreau grew from the French seeds of a plant indigenous to America. Each squash ended up weighing hundreds of pounds, and a man who bought one of them planned to sell the seeds for ten cents apiece. Thoreau tells his listeners they grew "in that corner of my garden," which, as we begin to understand, welcomes the prophetic seeds of nature. Eventually, the entire garden is filled with crops, representing a mystical transformation of the private garden of his mind to all of nature. Emphasizing the mysticism of nature, more incomprehensible through vigorous study and great reverence than through idle supposition, he shows us the miracle of the seed. "Though I do not believe that a plant will spring up where no seed has been, I have great faith in a seed . . . Convince me that you have a seed there, and I am prepared to expect wonders."[144] Here he echoes his expectations for John Brown, now moved from the temporal to the eternal rhythms of nature.

Case notes, "We have only fairly recently begun to realize (or perhaps remember) something that Thoreau learned in the course of his documenting his increasingly intimate relation to the natural world: that close observation is a mode of participating, that we are part of the world we would know."[145] If Thoreau's contemporaries had been able to perceive nature in a like manner, the whole world would be recognized as the garden it is. At the end of "Succession," he says, "Surely men love darkness better than light," prophetic language that echoes all the late essays.[146] Significantly, even though he concludes in the voice of the jeremiad, the final word in the last essay he composed is "light." Just as the blessed in Dante's paradise exist at the source of all light,[147] a proper transcendental dying is a stepping into the light, be it the triumphant sunrise that concludes *Walden,*[148] the light that dances with the scarlet oak leaves,[149] the light the wild apple springs joyfully into,[150] moonlight on a summer night,[151] the "morning light" of an autumn afternoon,[152] the minute blossoms of the white pine pointing toward the light of heaven,[153] or the immortal John Brown working in public "in the clearest light that shines on this land."[154]

The dark of the grave and of the minds of little men is the absence of light, but the pure idea, the graceful procession of the seasons, the life laid down for a principle, are a yearning into the light. The audience at the Middlesex Agricultural Society, which did not recognize the heroic natural world, doomed itself to a cowardly darkness; yet they, too, could have lived fully and died heroically into nature so that others might have striven into that light.

4

Artoosoqu' and the Button
From Inanimate Matter to Mystical State

The white pine, freshly cut piled by the side of the Charles Mile Road—is agreeable to walk beside—I like the smell of it all ready for the borers—and the rich light yellow color of the freshly split wood and the purple sap at the ends of the quarters—from which distill perfectly clear & crystalline tears—colorless and brilliant as diamonds—tears shed for the loss of a forest—in which is a world of light & purity—its life oozing out.

Human beings with whom I have no sympathy are far stranger to me than inanimate matter rocks or earth—Looking on the last I feel as if I were with my kindred.

—Henry David Thoreau, Journal,
March 24, 1853, and January 17, 1854

I

Thoreau's writing exhibits two elements of the physical/mystical as it relates to dying, and they usually work in tandem. The first is the transition state—the exact moment between life and death, the inexplicable shift from one to the other (see chapter 3). The second involves inanimate matter. Thoreau frequently gives life to the inanimate parts of nature, as when he compares the tears of John Brown and his wife to sweating rocks. He uses the physical/mystical mode throughout his Journal, and it is also an important aspect of *Walden*—for instance, when he describes giving life to his fire or the thawing sand of the railroad cut.[1]

Thoreau's posthumously published books, *The Maine Woods* (1864) and

Cape Cod (1865), include particularly concentrated forms of physical/mystical imagery. These books, which he was revising up until his death, were edited for publication by his sister Sophia and his friend William Ellery Channing. However, excerpts had been appearing in periodicals for more than a decade. He drafted "Ktaadn," the first section of *The Maine Woods,* in the fall of 1846 during his second year at Walden. Given that the section's physical/mystical sense was already fully developed at that early date, we cannot say that *The Maine Woods* and *Cape Cod* represent a late development in Thoreau's thinking about dying. Yet the theme's predominance in these books demonstrates how much Thoreau associated it with the parts of nature that were least hospitable to humankind. Like *A Week on the Concord and Merrimack Rivers, Walden,* his essays, and his Journal, they are predicated on close and careful awareness of the surrounding world. Yet *The Maine Woods* and *Cape Cod* speak particularly to physical objects and the relation between animate and inanimate. As Laura Dassow Walls notes in "Walking West, Gazing East," "ideas are material and materiality is ideal, and the distinction between matter and idea is yet another dichotomy that must be recognized and bracketed."[2]

In the *Walden* chapter titled "Where I Lived and What I Lived For," Thoreau writes, "If you stand right fronting and face to face with a fact, you will see the sun glimmer on both its surfaces, as if it were a cimeter [*sic*], and feel its sweet edge dividing you through heart and marrow, and so you will happily end your mortal career."[3] This enigmatic image is a pointed metaphor for dying well. But reality, which he believes few will reach through "the mud and slush of opinion," brings one to an irrefutable truth.[4] He makes truth temporal by representing it as an exact present moment, sharp as a scimitar. The moment has the sweetness of a clean and perfect death. Thoreau puns on "happily," which implies both "luckily" and "providentially" and suggests that another career awaits us after our "mortal" one. The rich passage evokes both animate life and the mysticism of dying.

The first element of the physical/mystical, the transition state, is a physical reality in the Journal entry that is the opening epigraph of this chapter. In Thoreau's beautiful paradox, the freshly cut pine trees are sensually pleasing, both in look and scent, as they lie "ready for the borers"—that is, await their transition into lumber. The "rich yellow" of the wood and "the purple color of the sap" connote flesh and blood, and suggestions of murder are reinforced by Thoreau's description of the distilling sap, which he compares to tears. By the end of the passage, what started out as a pleasant experience has become grief. Even though the trees are attractive in their cut state, that state is still the first step in their dying. At what point do they cease to be pines and become lumber? In the passage, the transition occurs at the introduction of the word "tears," which Thoreau attributes to both the trees themselves and to those who mourn them. In all living beings, the moment of transition between living and dying occurs instantaneously and in writing can be represented only by the anticipation created in the turn of a phrase.

In the second chapter epigraph, Thoreau contemplates a kind of life in inanimate matter. Turning his alienation from human companions and acquaintances into acceptance by the inanimate world, he constructs a kinship between himself and the rocks and the earth.[5] He often makes such links between his own body and the inanimate world. For example, in a December 15, 1850, Journal entry, he writes, "My feet are much nearer to foreign or inanimate matter or nature than my hands . . . They are more like the earth they tread on—they are more clod-like & lumpish &—I scarcely animate them."[6] His thoughts bear a certain resemblance to William Blake's poem "The Clod & the Pebble."[7] In both instances, an inanimate lump of earth takes on a kind of life. In Blake's poem, the clod has a voice; in Thoreau's entry, it has kinship with a living man. Thoreau also sets up another paradox: his hands, the more "human" part of his body, are animated by his living and thinking, whereas his semi-inanimate feet achieve a longed for kinship with the earth.

On May 2, 1851, Thoreau writes in his Journal about another mystical experience. A few days earlier, a dentist had pulled what was left of his teeth, and he was fitted for false ones. A decade later he refused all opiates when he was dying, but for the dental ordeal he had an ether-induced experience of altered consciousness.

> By taking the ether the other day I was convinced how far asunder a man could be separated from his senses. You are told it will make you unconscious—but no one can imagine what it is to be unconscious . . . The value of the experiment is that it does give you experience of an interval between one life and another—A greater space than you have ever travelled.[8]

Although Thoreau never used ether again, for the rest of the summer of 1851 he continued to experiment with another form of altered consciousness—the natural world by moonlight.[9] On June 11, Thoreau writes in his Journal, "It was necessary to see objects by moonlight—as well as by sunlight—to get a complete notion of them."[10] Like the mind, the physical world has two realities and exists somewhere between the two. In the same entry, he writes, "I do not know but I feel less vigorous at night—my legs will not carry me so far—as if night were less favorable to muscular exertion—weakened us somewhat as plants grow pale."[11] Like the unconsciousness induced by ether, the nighttime world separates us from our physical reality and adumbrates the experience of dying. To be conscious of becoming unconscious is glimpsing the space between the known world and something different. Dying is still on his mind when he writes, "Listen to music religiously as if were the last strain you might hear."[12]

In Thoreau's thinking there is an undercurrent of anxiety about the indefinable line that separates the life of day from the life of night. "Does perchance any of this pregnant air survive the dews of night—Can any of it be found remembering the sun of yesterday even in the morning hours? Does perchance some puff blast survive the night on elevated clearings surrounded by forest?"[13] Such questions raise others: how much consciousness must one have to apprehend unconsciousness? How much daylight must one know to experience the utter strangeness of the nighttime world? On the same night he hears a partridge drumming: "What singularly space penetrating filling sound—why am I never nearer to its source?"[14] This in-between of time and space is the location of dying—the ambiguity that he embraces by taking ether and going into the moonlight.

II

The physical/mystical is the sinew that binds together the three essays that compose *The Maine Woods*. Early in "Ktaadn," Thoreau introduces a major theme of the book, one he had clearly also been mulling in his Journal: the decimation of the white pine forests. Writing of the sawmills, he says, "Here your inch, your two and three inch stuff begin to be, and Mr. Sawyer marks off those spaces which decide the fate of so many prostrate forests."[15] The sentence hinges on the word "begin," because, though the trees have been cut down, they still retain their forest character. The loggers have made a first step in the carnage, but the sawmill will convert the forest into something completely unrecognizable. Thoreau describes coming across vast forests filled with trees, except that there are no white pines. Of these nothing remains but stumps; the valuable pines have been sacrificed for lumber in Massachusetts and elsewhere. The forest is in transition from life to death because its heart—the white pine—has been culled out. Throughout the book, Thoreau returns to the image of the white pine stumps. In the last section, "The Allegash and the East Branch," he writes of being appalled to hear loggers brag that they have cut down white pines so large that teams of oxen can stand on their stumps. "As if that were what the pine had grown for, to become the footstool of oxen."[16]

In the section "Chesuncook," Thoreau writes of admiring trees that fall naturally rather than being chopped down: "Sometimes an evergreen just fallen lay across the track with its rich burden of cones, looking, still, fuller of life than our trees in the most favorable positions."[17] Describing a tree in a natural state of transition, he also offers a mystical conundrum. If the tree has fallen, is it a dead tree? With so many cones, it seems more alive than many of the trees that are still standing in Concord. What, then, makes a tree alive? Left to fall naturally, the tree, which moves in slow time, remains both alive and dead. With its myriad cones, it exists in a long instant of transition.

Thoreau continues to explore this idea in a scene that is both comical and mystical. In the woods on a still night with their Penobscot guide, Joe Aitteon, the travelers hear "from the moss-clad aisles, a dull dry rushing sound, with a solid core to it . . . like the shutting of a door in some distant entry of the damp and shaggy wilderness."[18] Awed, they ask Aitteon in a whisper to tell them what it was, and the guide replies, "Tree fall." Here, Thoreau is playing with the old adage: does a tree falling in a forest make a noise if no one is there to hear it? But the moment is also a physical/mystical experience. A tree falling is a physical dying, but the uncanny enters into the mysterious sound of its dying.

One of Thoreau's most beautiful passages about the transition between living and dying appears in the trout fishing scenes in "Ktaadn." As some of the party set up camp for the night, Thoreau and a few others find left-behind birch fishing poles and go out in the boat to fish in a fast-moving stream flowing down from Mount Katahdin. "Speckled trout and silvery roach" quickly fall upon their bait, and the men toss the hooked fish onto the bank, from where they slither back into the water. Eventually Thoreau loses his hook so stands on the shore as the fish are thrown to him.

Speaking of himself in the third person to give primacy to the fish rather than to the anglers, he describes the physical experience of being among the dying fish. "They fell in a perfect shower around him—sometimes, wet and slippery, full in his face and bosom, as his arms were outstretched to receive them." This might merely be a comic set piece if Thoreau did not also give us the dazzling beauty of the sundown scene: "The fish, while yet alive, . . . glistened like the fairest flowers, the product of primitive rivers, and he could hardly trust his senses . . . that these jewels should have swam away in that Aboljacknagesic water for so long, so many dark ages . . . made beautiful the Lord only knows why to swim there!"[19] As with the beautiful clam shell left "tenantless" (discussed in chapter 2), the eland skin (discussed in chapter 3), and the pines in the Journal entry that opens this chapter, an extraordinary sensual beauty clings to the dying of natural objects. This beauty is transient; once the fish are out of the water, they are "bright fluviatile flowers" only in the moments in which they are dying, and only during this moment of transition can human eyes behold the glory nature has made for no reason that we can understand.[20]

Thoreau writes about awaking that night to wonder if he hadn't dreamed the entire experience. He decides to get up and go out to fishing again. "There stood Ktaadn with distinct and cloudless outline in the moonlight . . . The speckled trout and the silvery roach . . . sped swiftly through the moonlight air, describing bright arcs on the dark side of Kta-adn."[21] This beautiful yet uncanny passage evokes the question of what is animate or inanimate. Both before and later in the chapter, the inanimate mountain, partially obscured by clouds, finally stands out distinctly in the moonlight. Again, Thoreau avoids using the first person; the fish appear to fly across the outline of the mountain of their own volition. Are these "silvery arcs" alive? Technically, while the fish are still on the line, they are alive—but this is not a technical passage. Thoreau, the nameless speaker, we know is animate, the great rock of the mountain is inanimate, but passing between the two are silver arcs of timelessness itself, instantaneous transitions between animate and inanimate.

The moose-killing scene in "Chesuncook" is as shocking as the "Ktaadn" fishing scenes are magical, yet it evokes the same sense of transition. Aitteon shoots at a cow moose and her calf while Thoreau the naturalist is "plucking the seeds of the great round-leaved orchis." Thoreau tells us, "Joe exclaimed from the stream that he had found the cow moose lying dead, but quite warm, in the middle of the stream."[22] With difficulty, Thoreau and the guide drag the dead moose by her ears, for her "long nose [was] frequently sticking to the bottom," a horrifying moment reminiscent of the scene in Nathaniel Hawthorne's *The Blithedale Romance* when Zenobia's body is fished out of the river.[23] Is the corpse they are dragging still a moose? In the moments after becoming inanimate matter, she is still creaturely. Thoreau emphasizes her female attributes to heighten the sense of continued lifelike attributes, even as she is butchered. The guide begins to skin the animal while Thoreau watches: "a tragical business it was,—to see that still warm and palpitating body pierced with a knife, to see the warm milk stream from the rent udder, and the ghastly naked red carcass appearing from within its seemly robe, which was meant to hide it."[24] He is punning on the word "hide," but that does not lessen the hideousness of what he sees. Using the heroic narrative to evoke terror and pity and the sentimental narrative to emphasize the moose's motherhood, he modifies the adjective "naked" with the adverb "ghastly." We must not underestimate Thoreau's nineteenth-century sensibilities: female nudity is a horrifying concept. Warm blood mixed with warm milk is something no man should see; and by witnessing the baring of the naked red female, Thoreau is participating in a kind of rape. He emphasizes his own guilt by measuring the carcass—erroneously, as it turns out—and eating her flesh, which he says "tasted like tender beef, . . . sometimes like veal," suggesting her innocence.[25] He also says of moose in general that shooting them is like shooting a neighbor's horses, for they are "God's own horses, poor timid creatures."[26]

After the death of the moose, the excursion is partially ruined for Thoreau. "I . . . felt myself the coarser for this part of my woodland experience, and was reminded that life should be lived as daintily and tenderly as one would pluck a flower."[27] The moose's murder informs the rest of the chapter, particularly in relation to the despoliation of the white pine. He writes, "Every creature is better alive than dead, men and moose and pine-trees, and he who understands it aright will rather preserve its life than destroy it."[28] By referring to the pine tree as a "creature," he is giving it agency—a remarkable way to look at a tree. This agency, however, is what makes the pines' destruction so vile because it means that their death is on the same level as that of an animal or a human. Admitting that "Nature looked sternly upon me" after the death of the moose, he then immediately turns to the pines: "Strange that so few ever come to the woods to see how the

pine lives and grows and spires, lifting its evergreen arms to the light."
When he asks rhetorically if the lumberman is the true friend of the pine,
he answers definitively, "No! no! it is the poet; it is he who makes the truest
use of the pine," reminding himself of his own higher calling.[29]

Just as Thoreau makes the death of the moose more graphic and horrible
by emphasizing its femaleness, Thoreau feminizes the pine tree. The poet,
unlike the lumberman, "does not fondle [the pine] with an axe, nor tickle
it with a saw, nor stroke it with a plane—who knows whether its heart is
false without cutting into it."[30] This is a nineteenth-century way of describing a man with a prostitute, made more shocking because the lumberman
who has been intimate with the tree then cuts her open to inspect her
heart.[31] As the hunter rapes the moose, so the lumberman prostitutes the
white pine—the very femaleness of the animal and tree emphasizes their
helplessness. When speaking of the man "who has bought the stumpage
of the township," Thoreau writes, "All the pines shudder and heave a sigh
when *that* man steps on the forest floor."[32] This passage gives the sense of
a whole congregation of powerless women about to fall prey to a lustful,
avaricious man. The writer is making the pines human but is hinting at
their inanimacy as well. About the time Thoreau drafted "Chesuncook,"
he wrote in his Journal, "I mistook the creaking of a tree in the woods the
other day for the scream of a hawk. How numerous the resemblances of
the animate to the inanimate!"[33] In Thoreau's vision, the pines shudder, as
the rocks sweat, and Captain and Mrs. Brown weep.

III

In "Ktaadn," Thoreau takes a preliminary late-afternoon climb up one side
of the mountain. A major theme in the chapter is the life of rocks, and
in that first climb Thoreau tries to pastoralize them, though as he climbs
higher, they become stranger. As he comes up the side of the mountain,
"gray, silent rocks were the flocks and herds that pastured, chewing a rocky
cud at sunset."[34] Just previously he has called the stunted trees around him
a "garden," another attempt to turn this daunting landscape into a Concord meadow. Yet his domesticating words increase the alien nature of the
landscape. A stunted forest and bare rock outlined against the sunset are
emphatically not a welcoming scene but a prelude to the disconnect and

ultimate connection he will experience with inanimate matter as he climbs higher.[35]

In the night that separates his two climbs up Katahdin, Thoreau has a nightmare. His cries awaken the others at midnight, and Thoreau springs from his bed of twigs "thinking the world on fire."[36] This sense of alienation from the known world anticipates what Thoreau will experience on the mountain his second day. That morning, all the men begin to climb Katahdin, but Thoreau soon far outpaces the others, moving beyond the stunted trees and into a world of rocks, "as if sometime it had rained rocks and they lay as they fell . . . leaning on each other." This time, rather than pastoralizing the rocks, he anthropomorphizes them. Yet he immediately drops that simile to get at their true life: "They were the raw materials of a planet dropped from an unseen quarry."[37]

In the *Walden* chapter "Spring," nature is "sportive" and creative, spewing life forms in the shape of the thawing clay of the railroad cut. In "Ktaadn," however, nature is rougher and more primeval. Once again Thoreau is high in the clouds, as he was in *A Week*'s "Tuesday"; but this time the clouds don't create a sense of heightened wonder. Instead, he is "deep within the hostile ranks of clouds, and all objects were obscured by them."[38] Just sentences before, he had invested the rocks with human qualities; now they begin to rob him of his humanity. "It was vast, Titanic, such as man never inhabits. Some part of the beholder, even some vital part, seems to escape through the loose grating of his ribs . . . and Nature pilfers him of some of his divine faculties."[39] The rocks not only begin to leech away his human heart but also rob him of all pretense of theomorphism. The idea that he is made in the image of God becomes meaningless in an inanimate world.

Notably, in this inimical and inanimate world, Thoreau gives nature a voice. She asks, "Why came ye here before your time?"[40] Because matter personifies the natural world, Thoreau, in giving it a voice through nature, is giving this inanimate place its own voice. The rocks seem to speak for nature, admonishing the climber for venturing into a world not yet prepared for human habitation. Thoreau notes that the Indians, whom he believes have an especially close bond to nature, never climb steep, rocky places but revere them from a distance: "their tops are sacred and mysterious tracts."[41] He believes that nature does not want him here either and imagines that she asks, "Why seek me when I have not called thee, and then complain because you find me but a stepmother?"[42] Her question emphasizes his solitary state. Thoreau is cut off from his companions by distance and from nature as he has, till now, known her—benign, loving, and indulgent. The growing cloud cover emphasizes his dangerous solitude, so eventually he climbs back down to his companions to puzzle out what he has experienced. On his way he encounters, here and there, a stray sparrow, "unable to command its course like a fragment of gray rock blown off by the wind."[43] By likening the birds to inanimate rock, he, by inference, compares himself to a piece of rock falling down the mountainside, so altered is he by his experience.

On their way back from the mountain the men cross a burnt-over forest, where blueberry bushes and young poplars are coming up amid the fallen timber. The scene feels familiar to Thoreau, recalling a burnt-woods-going-to-meadow he has seen in Concord, but he realizes no man is the proprietor of this kind of country. In acclimating himself to the lack of ties this place has to man, he writes one of his most difficult paradoxes: "And yet we have not seen pure Nature unless we see her thus vast and drear and inhuman, though in the midst of cities."[44] The first part of the sentence is in keeping with what comes before: he feels he has undergone the primeval experience of pre-animal and -plant nature in his ascent of Katahdin. But how can one experience this kind of nature in a crowded city? The nature he refers to as "vast and drear and inhuman" is the unanimated part of the globe, which includes the human body minus the "vital" or "divine" part.[45] A city is a vast aggregate of bodies, each as strange to him as his own. He writes, "I fear not spirits, ghosts, of which I am one . . . but I fear bodies, I tremble to meet them."[46]

Once again Thoreau shifts to the third person, this time to give primacy to pure, unanimated matter: "It was Matter, vast terrific,—not his Mother Earth . . . not for him to tread on or be buried in,—no, it were being too familiar even to let his bones lie there."[47] By capitalizing the word *matter*, Thoreau makes it nature's principal avatar in the forbidding world of Katahdin. In the pages leading up to this revelation, he has kept trying to understand the "Titan" possessing him and the "Titanic" in nature.[48] Now he sees that this titanic entity is matter itself and understands that he must integrate this new knowledge into human living and dying. Because of its power, a man cannot be too familiar with matter, even the matter that comprises his own body. Yet he must seek to come to terms with it and consequently his demand for contact: "Think of our life in nature,—daily to be shown matter, to come in contact with it,—rocks, trees, wind on our cheeks!"[49]

In another significant passage, this time in the chapter "The Allegash," Thoreau again gives life to inanimate matter. He writes that he, his companion, and their Penobscot guide Joe Polis are asleep in "a dense and damp spruce and fir wood," absolutely dark except for their fire. Thoreau awakens after midnight and discovers that phosphorescent wood is gleaming in the fire, the first such wood he has ever seen—"a perfectly regular elliptical ring of light . . . fully as bright as the fire, but a white and slumbering light."[50] The wood is dead, he emphasizes, and the white light is ghostlike. Thoreau cuts some pieces to show his companion, and "they lit up the inside of my hand, revealing the lines and wrinkles." He goes on to say, "It could hardly have thrilled me more if it had taken the form of letters, or the human face."[51] The next morning Polis tells them that the Penobscot word for this otherworldly light is *Artoosoqu'*. Uninterested in the scientific explanation of the phenomenon, Thoreau "rejoice[s] in that light as if it had been a fellow-creature."[52] The Artoosoqu' makes him believe that "the woods [are] not tenantless, but choke-full of honest spirits as good as myself any day."[53]

This experience highlights Thoreau's relations with his Penobscot guides. As the historian John J. Kucich notes, the discovery of the Artoosoqu' was preceded, earlier in the evening, by a story that Polis told the the two white men. Kucich writes,

> *The Maine Woods* is . . . a powerful record of traditional Penobscot ped-agogy. Aitteon and Polis revealed some of their traditions and rituals, waiting as Indian teachers typically did, for the right circumstance to summon an appropriate story and then carefully gauging its effect. When Thoreau clearly wasn't ready, as when Polis told of Klose-ber-beh's killing of a moose that became Mount Kineo, the story may have taken effect. What follows that evening is Thoreau's revelation about phosphorescent wood and his newfound respect for the depths of Indian knowledge.[54]

According to Kucich, the guides taught Thoreau how to experience the natural world even more intimately: "By carefully attending to the land-scape, by focusing on the flora, fauna, and geology, that met his gaze, Thoreau managed (if only temporarily and partially) to escape the narrow ideological perspective of nineteenth-century expansionism and open himself to alternative ways of understanding this environment."[55]

Thoreau's approach to the life of inanimate matter vis-à-vis the phosphorescent wood seems different from that of the approach he expressed in "Ktaadn." In the scene in "The Allegash," his discovery of his kinship with the utterly alien does not involve a painful, drawn-out process. Yet despite the different process, the recognition is the same. The cold coals light up his hand, drawing all its particulars into relief, as though the dead pieces of wood have animated it. Thoreau recognizes this strange light as a fellow being because it glows as mysteriously as a person lives—and as briefly, for on the next night the light has vanished from the wood.

In "Ktaadn" the writer establishes his kinship with earth, rocks, trees, and wind. In *Walden* he personifies fire. But the Artoosoqu' is a symbol for the life in all inanimate matter. Beyond science, beyond the ontological puzzle he struggled with on Katahdin, this light glows not only in his hand but in his imagination. Once again, Thoreau has made contact. The cold light of the phosphorescent wood is the moon to the fire's sun, briefly animating the strangeness of the nighttime wilderness and its own existence.

IV

Laura Dassow Walls notes that "one enters Thoreau's [*Cape Cod*] through the scene of a shipwreck, and its pages are haunted by his morbid and graphic descriptions of dead bodies and living 'wreckers' who see in corpses nothing but commodity."[56] In 1849 the brig *St. John* wrecked on the shores of the Cape Cod town of Cohasset, and Thoreau began his last book with a description of the aftermath of that wreck. A year later he would see the remnants of the wreck of the *Elizabeth* on the shores of New York's Fire Island; and though he never mentions the second wreck by name, it informs his descriptions of shipwreck throughout the book. Thoreau arrived at Point O' Woods, a town on the island, on July 24, 1850, five days after the ship had run aground on a hidden sandbar during a combined nor'easter and early-season hurricane. Among those killed in the wreck were transcendentalist Margaret Fuller; her husband, the marquis Giovanni Angelo Ossoli; and their two-year-old son. Emerson had given Thoreau seventy dollars and sent him to recover Fuller's effects, particularly the manuscript of her book about the Italian revolution. During his stay,

Thoreau visited the grave of Fuller's son (the parents' bodies were never found), but all he brought back was a brass button he tore from the Republican Guard jacket of Fuller's husband.[57] From Concord, he wrote to his friend, Harrison Blake: "I have in my pocket a button I ripped off the coat of the Marquis Ossoli on the seashore the other day. Held up, it intercepts the light,—an actual button,—and yet all the life it is connected with is less substantial to me, and interests me less, than my faintest dream."[58]

Why did he keep the button? He had never met Ossoli and was not a close friend of Fuller's. In his letter, he doesn't tell Blake how he learned that the button was Ossoli's but implies that the fact had made itself known to him in some inexplicable way.[59] Moreover, he retells the story to himself in his Journal: "I have in my pocket a button which I ripped off the coat of the Marquis Ossoli, an *actual* button, so-called." Thoreau's italics emphasize his pun. In the mid-nineteenth century, the meaning of *actual* was changing from "of the present time" to "something real." Thoreau's choice of "so-called" is a kind of distress signal: he is not so much asking if the button is real but wondering if it has meaning beyond the purely inanimate. What is its relation to the light it reflects? How is it connected to the animate world? Does it have any link to the world of the spirit? As Fuller's biographer John Matteson notes, "the small souvenir made him think about the strangeness of a world in which inanimate objects survive and the living could vanish overnight."[60]

In my view, buttons became so potent a symbol of drowning for Thoreau that Ossoli's absorbed his consciousness as he worked on his tale of the wrecks on Cape Cod. In an October 26, 1851, Journal entry, written two years after the wreck of the *St. John*, a year after the wreck of the *Elizabeth*, and while he was at work on the early sections of *Cape Cod*, he says,

> I awoke this morning to infinite regret. In my dream I had been riding—but the horses bit . . . each other and occasioned endless trouble and anxiety & it was my employment to hold their heads apart. Next I sailed over the sea in a small vessel such as the Northmen used—as it were to the bay of Funday & thence overland I sailed . . . Again I was in my own small pleasure boat—learning to sail on the sea—& I raised my sail before my anchor which I dragged far into the sea—I saw the buttons which had come off the coats of drowned men.[61]

The connection between buttons and the drowned doesn't end here. Using a telescoping technique, he combines the two trips he made with

Channing in October 1849 and July 1853 into one narrative—the story of the 1849 trip—and then jumps ahead to his solitary June 1850 excursion. He does this in the first chapter of *Cape Cod,* returning to Cohasset, the scene of the wreck of the *St. John,* on a calm, hot day and bathing in a rocky tide pool. While writing about this interlude, he tells us how cold the water is, even on a hot day, and notes that the temperature of the water, as much as the power of the surf, can kill a shipwrecked victim. He continues, "The stripe of barnacles just above the weeds . . . lay along the seams of the rock like buttons on a waistcoat."[62] He remains consciously aware of the connections he is making between shipwrecks and buttons. As late as chapter 8, "The Highland Light," he describes a 1741 French coin he finds on the beach: "Of course, I thought it was the same old button I had found so many times, but my knife soon showed the silver."[63] The button represents both a transition state (a manmade object on a living man moving to pure thingness, reflecting the light but remaining mute) and the special life of inanimate matter, which, like the bones of the drowned on the sea floor, refuses to remain quiet to the imagination.

V

One of the most devastating images from *Cape Cod* occurs in the first pages—the description of the drowned Irish girl who had been coming to America to go into service. By way of her corpse, Thoreau begins his meditation on the transition of animate to inanimate matter: "I saw . . . one livid, swollen, and mangled body of a drowned girl . . . to which some rags still adhered, with a string, half concealed by the flesh about its swollen neck."[64] Note that, in the transition from this entity he acknowledges as a "girl," he shifts to something he identifies as "it." He continues to establish this inanimacy by describing the body as "the coiled-up wreck of a human hulk, gashed by rocks or fishes . . . with wide-open and staring eyes, yet lusterless, dead-lights; or like the cabin windows of a stranded vessel, filled with sand."[65] In his account, the body takes on the characteristics of a wrecked ship, both lifeless objects with "eyes" that look out on nothing.

Thoreau is as interested in the reactions of the people at the site of the wreck as he is in the wreck itself. He listens to the ship's mate, "a slim looking youth, who spoke of the captain as the master, and seemed a little excited." The young man explains that when he jumped into one of the lifeboats, it lurched and filled with water, and the weight of the swamped boat broke the painter. The mate's excitement is what we might today call survivor's guilt. Thoreau listens to the story sympathetically but notices that not all the listeners respond in the same manner. One says, " 'Well, I don't see but he tells a straight story enough. You see, the weight of the water broke the painter. A boat full of water is very heavy,' and so on, in a loud and importantly earnest tone, as if he had a bet depending on it, but no humane interest in the matter."[66] In contrast to this man's mood of pure spectatorship, Thoreau's reaction is sensitive and understanding.

Again Thoreau uses the idea of moving west as moving into dying. He says of the *St. John*'s victims, "I saw their empty hulks come to land; but they themselves, meanwhile, were cast upon some shore further west, toward which we are all tending."[67] Some critics argue that Thoreau's language here mocks sentimental newspaper accounts; but as I have already discussed, he does create in the body of his work the idea of heaven, whether or not he believed in it. By having the Irish emigrants move "further west," he puts them into the category of the autumn light in his essay "Walking." By noting that we are all tending west, he reinforces the physical/mystical idea that our lives exist in a state of transition between living and dying. In this sense, all of Cape Cod is in a transition state. Returning to the site of the wreck on a warm day during the following summer, Thoreau says, "Nor could I believe that the bones of many a shipwrecked man were buried in that pure sand."[68] In other words, as the scholar Christopher A. Dustin writes,

> Thoreau is moved to wonder not just *that* any had been saved, but in what sense. What could it mean to be "saved" when all matter (including our own bodies) is destined only for salvage or when even the living are mere "remains"? . . . Thoreau is surprised not just by the mere fact that some human individuals had survived the wreck; he is also moved by the sense that *how* they were saved seems indistinguishable from the way the seaweed and other "smaller fragments" were saved by the wreckers.[69]

Most of the narrative echoes the effects of the storm that wrecked the *St. John*. In their northward travel up the cape, Thoreau and Channing are constantly reminded of the storm, whether by wind, rain, or heavy surf. Thoreau continues to draw a connection between wrecked bodies and wrecked ships, pointing out that the wreckers themselves (the term given to men who comb the shore after wrecks, searching for valuables, timber, and fertilizing seaweed) are so weathered that they resemble the ships they scavenge. "We soon met one of these wreckers . . . with a bleached and weather-beaten face, within whose wrinkles I distinguished no particular feature. It was like an old sail, endowed with life." Yet Thoreau also tells us that the wrecker "is the true monarch of the beach . . . and he is as much identified with it as a sea-bird."[70]

The book is informed to a lesser degree by another sea disaster, the wreck of the *Franklin*. Thoreau's contemporaries were familiar with the tale: all of the region's newspapers had carried articles about a letter discovered in a valise, which seemed to prove that the captain had wrecked the ship deliberately, by order of the owners. The *Franklin* was a particularly advantageous wreck for those ashore because of the vast numbers of young fruit trees and seeds that had washed up from it. During Thoreau and Channing's travels, locals pointed out the fruit and vegetables growing in the sandy soil. In *Cape Cod*'s mostly comic chapter, "The Wellfleet Oysterman," the old man quizzes them in his garden, "making us tell him the names of the vegetables he had raised from seeds that came out of the *Franklin*."[71] As I have shown in chapter 3, seeds are significant emblems of Thoreau's idea of dying and rebirth, or continuous living. From crime, death, and destruction come flourishing life. Yet the violence of the *Franklin*'s wreck is evident in the old man's laconic description, which eerily echoes the drowning of Margaret Fuller: "the boat was able to reach them, and it saved all that were left, but one woman."[72] The sense that death brings about fertility is also apparent in the sea itself: "Schools of Menhaden rippled the surface, scarcely to be distinguished from clouds . . . such was [the sea's] inexhaustible fertility."[73] Once again life and death exist in a transition state between animate and inanimate. This fertility coming out of death is reminiscent of the "Spring" chapter in *Walden*, particularly in Thoreau's description of the rotting horse, which cheers him with the health of nature.[74]

Cape Cod, however, is much darker than either *Walden* or the nature essays are. "The walker here must soon eat his heart," not only because of the desolation of the landscape but also because of his knowledge of the carnage beneath the sea.[75] In a description reminiscent of his climb up Katahdin, Thoreau writes of "barren heaths of poverty-grass for heather."[76] The grass represents a transition between living and dead vegetation: "In summer, if the poverty-grass grows . . . in a bleak position . . . the northern or exposed half of the tuft is sometimes all black and dead, like an oven-broom, while the opposite half is yellow with blossoms, the whole hillside thus presenting a remarkable contrast."[77] The plant, both alive and dead, is a metaphor for his vision of Cape Cod. Along the same stretch of beach he finds buried in the sand a stoppered bottle of ale, tastes it, and pours out the rest. He muses, "Man himself was like a half-emptied bottle of pale ale, which time has drunk so far . . . drifting about in the ocean of circumstances but destined to . . . be spilled amid the sands of a distant shore."[78] In other words, we are all both wreckers and wrecks: "this same placid Ocean . . . will toss and tear the rag of a man's body like the father of mad bulls, and his relatives may be seen seeking the remnants for weeks along the strand."[79]

Thoreau vividly evokes the transition from living sailor to inanimate matter in his description of the "Humane-houses" or "Charity-houses" erected by the municipal government to provide shelter for shipwrecked sailors. After reading about them in their old guidebooks, Thoreau and Channing come across one, a dilapidated hut that seems "but a stage to the grave." The man assigned to care for the house has not maintained it, for he "thinks that storms and shipwrecks are all over."[80] The door hasp has rusted shut. The only way to see inside is to look through a knothole "without knowing how many shipwrecked men's bones we might see." Eventually, however, "things began to take shape to our vision where there was nothing but emptiness—and we obtained the long-wished for insight."[81] Here Thoreau contrasts the inhumanity of man—the barrenness of his charity—with the unintentionality of nature.

One could argue that shipwreck is the true topic of *Cape Cod,* both literally and figuratively. From the moment a ship founders until the moment, perhaps centuries later, when its inanimate and once animate parts disappear into the sea, a shipwreck represents transition. At the beginning of the book, Thoreau gives precedence to the souls of the shipwrecked emigrants; near the end he reconsiders their bones. In the course of his hike up the cape he begins to see that, for humans, the transition to inanimate matter reverberates like the aftermath of the storm that wrecked the *St. John.* "There are more consequences to a shipwreck than the underwriters notice. The Gulf Stream may return some to their native shores, or drop them in some out-of-the-way cave of Ocean, where time and the elements will write new riddles with their bones."[82]

VI

Just as Thoreau feminizes and thus humanizes the dead moose and the pine trees in *The Maine Woods,* he imagines Massachusetts as the warrior goddess Athena and sees Cape Cod as her "bare and bended arm," "behind which the State stands on her guard . . . boxing with the northeast storms and ever and anon, heaving up her Atlantic adversary from the lap of earth."[83] In describing this battle between land and sea, he anticipates the slow back-and-forth time he constructs in his lecture "The Succession of Forest Trees." "The ocean has, in the course of time, eaten out Boston harbor and other bays in the mainland, and . . . the minute fragments have been deposited by the currents at a distance from the shore, and formed this sand-bank."[84] Though he begins and ends the book with an image of Cape Cod as a bended arm, he also alludes to the cape as a body in itself, giving further life to the inanimate. "There are many holes and rents in this weather-beaten garment . . . which reveal the naked flesh of the Cape, and its extremity is completely bare."[85] Later, he again uses human imagery to describe the inanimate female body of the cape: "This sand-bank—the backbone of the Cape—which runs the whole length of the forearm . . . and beyond this stretched the unwearied and illimitable ocean."[86]

Cape Cod is also a classically influenced book about the epic struggle between land and sea. As a landsman himself, Thoreau is on Athena's side, but he admires the power of the sea: "I wished to see that seashore where men's works are wrecks . . . where the ocean is land-lord as well as sea-lord . . . where the crumbling land is only invalid, or at best is but dry land, and that is all you can say of it."[87] Though he usually portrays the land as holding its own, he reminds us that the sea not only has the power to undress the female land but was its primordial origin: "Before the land rose out of the ocean and became *dry* land, chaos reigned; and in between high and low water mark, where she is partially disrobed and rising, a sort of chaos reigns still."[88]

The inanimate features of this inhospitable place take on animate as well as classical attributes. In a reference to the myth of the lost island of Atlantis, Thoreau says, "There must be something monstrous, . . . more awful than its imagined bottomlessness, . . . a drowned continent, . . . like the body of a drowned man."[89] Here he addresses his overwhelming horror at the carnage of the sea. As Dustin notes, "human bodies, weeds, stranded hulks—it is all of a piece in Thoreau's description. Of course it is important to recognize that what Thoreau is describing is not simply a scene as he sees it. His description is a reflection of . . . the way those around him relate to the 'matter' of the wreck."[90]

In the "Spring" chapter of *Walden,* Thoreau writes, "At the same time that we are earnest to explore and learn all things, we require that all things be mysterious and unexplorable, that land and sea be infinitely wild, unsurveyed and unfathomed because unfathomable."[91] At the edge of the ocean, he truly learns what it means for nature to be unfathomable. Walls notes, "This insight that forces the survivor to wrest from death an existential beauty could be applied to all his work after the death of his brother, including *Walden;* but articulating this terrible truth required the tremendous scale shift from kettle pond to world ocean."[92]

As they walk up Cape Cod, Thoreau and Channing come upon some beached blackfish, or orcas, "smooth and shining black, like India-rubber, and remarkably simple and lumpish forms for animated creatures."[93] Like so much else tossed up by the sea, however, the whales are dead. The two men study only the "forms" because the blackfish are wrecks too. Dustin writes, "In the face of nature's wildness, it seems we must all be 'shipwrecked' into and out of life."[94] To contain this wildness, Thoreau tries to liken the sea and wind to a farmhouse dog: "Instead of having a dog to growl before your door, to have an Atlantic Ocean to growl for a whole Cape!" Yet just as he dismisses his pastoralizing on Katahdin, he dismisses this domestic comparison: "On the whole, we were glad of the storm, which would show us the ocean in its angriest mood."[95]

Despite his fascination with the angry ocean, Thoreau's sympathies remain with the land: "The sea sends its rapacious east wind to rob the land, but before the former has got far with its prey, the land sends its honest west wind to recover some of its own."[96] Once again, both sea and land have animate qualities: the sea carnivorous, the land a good shepherd. As the book progresses, the writer begins to see the kinship between inlanders like himself and the inhabitants of the shore. He begins by admiring the ocean at its stormiest because it is so "sublimely dreary," sympathizing more with the spirit of inanimate nature than with human loss.[97] Later he comes to understand the cape inhabitants, who are, despite their proximity to the sea, land creatures like himself. "The stranger and the inhabitant view the shore with very different eyes. The former have come to see and admire the ocean in a storm; but the latter looks on it as the scene where his nearest relatives were wrecked."[98] The cape itself, as much as the adversarial ocean, engages him—this thin, strong arm defending the land from an indifferent sea. The cape is like and not like a live thing; and in trying to understand its "thingness," Thoreau tries to understand his own relationship to the seashore. "I got the Cape under me, as much as if I were riding it bareback . . . out of doors, huge and real, Cape Cod, . . . the thing itself."[99]

Early in *Cape Cod,* Thoreau says there is only ocean between himself and Europe. The last sentence of the book is "A man may stand here and put all America behind him."[100] Many critics have read this sentence as part of Thoreau's ongoing critique of his country. But if Thoreau is disowning his country and looking eastward (quite a departure for a man who so frequently turns westward), what exactly is he looking toward? He has never had any use for modern Europe.

Walls suggests that Thoreau is looking east toward the origins of the eastern philosophies and cosmologies that he so admired.[101] My interpretation is different. In *Walden,* he writes, "Start now on the farthest western way, which does not pause at the Mississippi or the Pacific, nor conduct toward a worn-out China or Japan but leads on."[102] I believe the ending of *Cape Cod* implies, in Thoreau's reinforced sense of landedness, that he has become a lookout for Athena's fighting arm, a kind of human lighthouse. He looks out on the sea warily and with respect, ever on the alert, ever mindful, just as he was at Walden. Before he ends the book, he predicts that the cape will someday become a fashionable resort, "but this shore will never be more attractive than it is now."[103] "Attractive" is an interesting choice of adjective. It implies the work of making oneself appealing to another as opposed to the indifferent and sublime grandeur he's been describing all along. Yet the adjective, in feminizing the cape, also humanizes it, despite its dearth, wreckage, and death. Is the mystery of the light glinting off a stray brass button beautiful? Like phosphorescent wood, the light reflected by the button shows the mystery and the life of the inanimate world.

5

"As long as she cracks she holds"
Thoreau's Dying as His Final Text

Human beings are rarely simply passive victims of death. They are actors even if they are the diers; they prepare for death, imagine it, risk it, endure it, seek to understand it.

—DREW GILPIN FAUST, *This Republic of Suffering: Death and the American Civil War*

I

In earlier episodes of near-fatal illness, Thoreau was afflicted by lethargy and despair. In contrast, his final illness was marked by industry, cheerfulness, and warmth—a surprise to observers outside his immediate family, who were used to seeing him as the village ne'er-do-well and misanthrope. In 1861, as Thoreau came to realize that this illness would be his last, he began constructing from his studies of dying a text that his survivors could easily read. His writings on dying as sentimental, heroic, and physical/mystical had grown primarily out of his nature studies. Now he incorporated these discoveries into his gradual but accelerated return to his family and community, a process that he had begun in 1848, when he left the Emerson household to rejoin his family's. The sentimental text of his dying was particularly meaningful to his last remaining sibling, his sister Sophia, who spent the fourteen years between her brother's death and her own rereading and disseminating this legacy.

Dying as a heroic act was a well-known trope in 1862, a particularly difficult year for the Union. As I have shown, Thoreau replaced his horror of physical death with his growing understanding of the heroism that inheres with the ongoing process of generation in nature. There is no true death in nature; rather, an ongoing process of ripening accompanies the planet through its eternal cyclical present. The autumnal falling of leaves and apples, birds' spring devouring of frog spawn, the annihilation of a stand of pine to make way for a stand of oak: all of these heroic deaths demonstrate one generation's willing nurture of the next.

Thoreau may have modeled his own dying on John Brown's behavior after his capture at Harpers Ferry. Realizing he could do more for the cause of abolition by dying, Brown refused last-minute attempts at rescue or efforts to commute his sentence to life imprisonment.[1] Thoreau, who also felt he had reached his own ripeness, his own "peculiar autumnal tint," refused any medical treatment that may have prolonged his life.[2] Likewise, just as Brown refused the comfort of words from what he perceived as a corrupt southern clergy, Thoreau refused the opiates that would have eased his pain but clouded his mind. Importantly, both men, up to their final moments, wrote copious, eloquent prose that they knew would have great impact. For Thoreau, Brown offered the rare human model of how to die as nature teaches.

The stoicism of Thoreau's dying was emphasized in Emerson's funeral eulogy, a speech that was later expanded into a lengthy essay in the *Atlantic Monthly*. Emerson's point of view had far greater influence than Thoreau's sister did; thus, his mythically stoic Thoreau took precedence over her sentimental version, especially in the decades after the Civil War, when sentimental readings began to fall out of favor. Though Thoreau himself left no record of sympathy with the Union dead, those who read his dying as a heroic text easily made that connection. He was as well known for his passionate (if intermittent) denunciations of slavery and wishy-washy northern abolitionism as he was for his philosophical and naturalist writings. Therefore, it was easy for readers to put him into the company of all those heroes who had died for the cause of freedom.

In addition to his sentimental and heroic versions, Thoreau clearly created a physical/mystical text of his dying. Nonetheless, this version has had the fewest readers. Perhaps the reason is related to an overall decline of interest in transcendentalism. By the beginning of the Civil War, it was no longer a significant literary and cultural movement but was seen as quaint and naïve, out of step with the times. Until the end of his life, however, Thoreau continued to call himself a transcendentalist, perhaps with more relish as fewer writers, poets, and intellectuals were willing to own the name.

While transition, or liminal, states were a basis of transcendental thought, no other transcendentalist devoted as many thoughts or pages to them as Thoreau did. During the war, most people—even Emerson— were unable to see time as an ontological puzzle unbound by clocks or railroad schedules. But on his death bed Thoreau continued his study of the present moment, a transition he refers to in *Walden* as the "meeting of two eternities" that cannot be identified or experienced until it has passed. In this sense, it has no existence except as a mystical state.[3] No season can ever be pinpointed: autumn contains the summer just passing, the winter coming, and the eventual return of spring. As he narrowed his seasonal observations to months, then weeks, then days, Thoreau still knew he would never capture the exact transition from one state to another except through written representations after the moment had passed.

As I discussed in chapter 4, Thoreau was most compelled by the transitional state of dying. At what point did a white pine or a moose cease to be pine or moose and become lumber or meat? In the essay, "Autumnal Tints," he describes the leaves of the scarlet oak, the last leaves of autumn, "lifted higher and higher, and sublimating more and more, putting off some earthiness and cultivating more intimacy with the light . . . have at length the least possible amount of earthly matter and . . . dance arm and arm with the light."[4] Like the leaves, Thoreau has shed most of his earthliness and is very close to death, but in spirit he is still alive, having his last dance with the light, even if his dancing means dictating from his pillow-propped chair and his light is his mother's parlor fire. Thin and wasted as the leaves, he still lives in the midst of dying—a state that is the inverse of traditional Christian mysticism, that in the midst of life one must always remember death. Thoreau invoked this liminal state when he wrote about Brown in the past tense, even before Brown had actually been hanged. Bronson Alcott, a Platonic mystic and fellow transcendentalist, did the same, publishing his own Thoreau eulogy, "The Forester" in the *Atlantic Monthly* just before Thoreau's actual death.

II

During his last months of life, Thoreau's dying reverberated among the "readers" of that text. Two of Louisa May Alcott's novels for adults, *Moods* (1864) and *Work: A Story of Experience* (1873), feature characters based on him—men who raised gardens, played the flute, fed birds from their hands, made birchbark baskets for berries, and, most importantly, died young, cheerfully and courageously, sacrificing themselves so that others might live.[5] When Nathaniel and Sophia Hawthorne returned to Concord from Europe in the early 1860s, their daughter Rose was terrified by the staring gray eyes and enormous nose of her father's friend, until Thoreau redeemed himself to her by "fall[ing] desperately ill." Once dead, he ever after became her companion when she "gathered a cardinal flower or any rare bloom."[6] Today, even the most glancing reader knows that, on his death bed, when asked if he could see the other side of the "dark river" he was approaching, Thoreau replied, "one world at a time."[7] His listener and the context may be forgotten, but the phrase has become a touchstone.

In *The Environmental Imagination,* Lawrence Buell notes that, unlike Emerson, Thoreau "has been seen much more as a great American *character,* on similar legendary and historical footing as Daniel Boone, Benjamin Franklin, and Abraham Lincoln."[8] The creation of this "character" was fully aided by Thoreau himself. While Buell is focusing on the perception that Thoreau is a moral exemplar of environmentalism even though much of his writing leans more toward transcendentalism, the idea that Thoreau's life and work were a process of artistic and moral self-definition also applies to his experience of his dying.

On May 20, 1862, Sophia Thoreau wrote to Daniel Ricketson:

> Profound joy mingles with my grief. I feel as if something very beautiful had happened, not death; although Henry is no longer with us . . . ' You ask for some particulars relating to Henry's illness. I feel like saying Henry was never affected, never reached by it. I never saw before saw such a manifestation of the power of spirit over matter. Very often I heard him tell his visitors that he enjoyed existence as much as ever. He remarked to me that there was as much comfort in perfect disease as in perfect health, the mind always conforming to the condition of the body.[9]

Thoreau himself had once written a similar letter to Ricketson, describing his father's deathbed in February 1859 and emphasizing the sense of humor that he and his father shared:

> Till within a week or ten days before he died he was hoping to see another spring, but he then discovered that this was a vain expectation, and, thinking he was dying, he took leave of us several times within a

week before his departure. Once or twice he expressed slight impatience at the delay. He was quite conscious to the last, and his death was so easy that, though we had all been sitting around the bed for an hour or more expecting that event (as we had sat before), he was gone at last almost before we were aware of it.[10]

Thoreau's earlier experiences of serious illness were not the triumph his final illness turned out to be. They felled him emotionally and creatively as well as physically, one of the best examples being the somatic lockjaw he suffered after his brother's death (see chapter 1). Another illness overtook him in the months after the publication of *Walden* in August 1854. Although this, like many of his ailments, was probably related to his incipient consumption, the bout had strange and uncharacteristic symptoms. In addition to suffering from lethargy and an inability to write, the great walker found that his legs were too weak to carry him far. This bizarre ailment lingered, with occasional abatements, for nearly two years. His biographer Robert D. Richardson, Jr., writes, "Emerson noted with alarm in June [1855] that Thoreau was feeble and languishing. Alcott thought he seemed shiftless for the first time. Channing noted that his cough was particularly bad that summer . . . In early October he visited Ricketson for a few days, compelled by his continued weakness to travel about the countryside by wagon."[11]

Thoreau wrote about this illness and depression sporadically in his Journal but discussed it more deeply in his letters to his longtime correspondent Harrison G. O. Blake. On June 27, 1855, he told Blake, "I have been sick and good for nothing but to lie on my back and wait for something to turn up, for two or three months. This has *compelled* me to postpone several things, among them writing to you, . . . not having brains adequate to such exertion. I should feel a little less ashamed if I could give any name to my disorder but I cannot . . . and I will not take the name of any disease in vain."[12]

Thoreau's connection between his ability to write and his ability to walk was familiar to all of his intimates. By 1850, he had set the pattern for the rest of his life: during most afternoons, in all weather, he would walk outdoors for several hours, taking brief field notes that he would later expand into Journal entries, sometimes several days' worth at one sitting.[13] In his funeral address, Emerson recalled, "He said he wanted every stride his legs made. The length of his stride uniformly made the length of his writing. If shut up in the house he did not write at all."[14] In his June 27 letter to Blake, Thoreau noted, "I expected in the winter to be deep in the woods of Maine in my canoe long before this, but I am so far from this I can only take a languid walk in Concord streets." He finished playfully yet ominously: "I thank you again and again for the encouragement your letters are to me. But I must stop this writing, or I shall have to pay for it."[15]

In letters, Thoreau continued to tell Blake about his weak legs, and on September 26, 1855, he wrote of once again hoping to align his creativity with nature after this long fallow period. "But I do not see how strength is to be got into my legs again. These months of feebleness have yielded few, if any, thoughts, though they may not have passed without serenity, such as our sluggish Musketaquid suggests. I hope that the harvest is to come." A few paragraphs later he recounts a dream that seems to bear out his anticipation: "I dreamed, last night, that I could vault over any height that pleased me. That was *something;* and I contemplated myself with a slight satisfaction in the morning for it."[16]

On April 10, 1856, as his long post-*Walden* illness was winding down, Thoreau wrote in his Journal about the last of the snow: "In the shade of walls and north hillsides and cool hollows in the woods, it is panting its life away . . . It is now advancing toward summer apace, and we seem to be reserved to taste its sweetness, but to perform what great deeds? Do we detect the reason why we also did not die on the approach of spring?"[17] The implication is that he has not completed his apprenticeship in nature: he cannot die, as he says in "A Plea for Captain John Brown," until he has learned to live.

All his life Thoreau's health had been fragile.[18] With a few well-known exceptions, this had rarely prevented him from being out of doors in all kinds of weather. The most popular version of his dying is that he caught cold counting tree rings on a wet, blustery day in 1860. Despite the severity of his cold, he refused to cancel his "Autumnal Tints" lecture in New Bedford later that week. The lecture and the traveling made him much worse, and he soon developed severe bronchitis, which kept him housebound the rest of the winter. He did not improve much in the spring but was able to resume some of his outdoor activities. Probably sensing that this was his final illness, he began trying to organize his vast notebooks into the manuscripts he had hoped to create from them: "The Succession of Trees,"

"Notes on Fruit," "Night and Moonlight." He may also have hoped to turn his massive notes on American Indians into a book.

As Thoreau's strength rapidly declined, his family, friends, and doctors urged him to travel to a different climate. He rejected the time and expense of Europe and the humidity of the West Indies and opted instead for Minnesota. Because none of his usual companions would accompany him, he chose Horace Mann, Jr., as a traveling companion Only seventeen years old, Mann had already proven himself to be a talented and mature botanist.[19]

Though Thoreau was able to do a significant amount of botanizing and observing, his health did not improve, and he and Mann returned to Concord earlier than scheduled. Once home, he seemed to rally again. He made a final visit to Ricketson in New Bedford in August, where his friend convinced him to sit for what has become known as the Dunshee ambrotype: the one in which he has a full beard and gaunt face. After he returned to Concord, walking became increasingly difficult for him, so Judge Samuel Hoar lent him a horse and buggy, and he and Sophia took nearly daily drives. Sophia was with him when he visited Walden for the last time, in September 1861. While his sister sketched, Thoreau gathered wild grapes, which he dropped one by one into the water. As autumn progressed, he developed pleurisy in addition to the consumption he was still calling bronchitis. No one except the ever-unrealistic Ricketson expected him to survive. Thoreau made his last Journal entry on November 3, 1861.

Knowing his time was short, the writer set aside his large projects and concentrated on what he could accomplish in a few months. For a weak, dying man, his output was astonishing. He revised his three Maine essays and his Cape Cod excursions for posthumous publication. He prepared four essays for the *Atlantic Monthly*, negotiated second editions of *Walden* and *A Week on the Concord and Merrimack Rivers*, and corrected the many printing errors that had appeared in the first edition of *A Week*. When he became too weak to hold a pencil, he dictated to Sophia.

Amazed by Thoreau's industry, friends and neighbors were also struck by his cheerfulness, tenderness, and humor. When he could no longer manage the stairs, family members brought his small cane bed (which he had put together for his Walden house) into the parlor. His mother noted that the room in no way resembled a sickroom; her son wanted it to be filled with books and flowers. When he heard children outside, he asked that they be brought in to visit him. An organ grinder playing an old song on the street brought him to tears, and he bid his mother to "give him some money!"[20]

Friends and townspeople visited often, bringing delicate food and news of the spring. The bluebird had always been Thoreau's harbinger of spring, and Emerson reported its arrival and shared regular bulletins about the state of the ice on the ponds. One day, as Emerson was arriving, Sam Staples, the man who had long ago jailed Thoreau overnight for not paying his poll tax, was just leaving. He told Emerson that he had "never spent an hour with more satisfaction. Never saw a man dying with so much pleasure and peace."[21] While the ice remained solid, Harrison Blake and Theo Brown skated from Worcester to Concord, taking part in warm and spirited conversations with their friend, though by this time he could only whisper. Brown later wrote to Ricketson about one of those visits: "We found him pretty low, but well enough to be up in his chair. He seemed glad to see us; said we had not come much too soon . . . His talk was up to the best I ever heard from him—the same depth of earnestness and the same infinite depth of fun going on at the same time."[22]

A few weeks before Thoreau's death, Grindell Reynolds, the Unitarian minister who had performed Thoreau's father's funeral and would later preside over Thoreau's, found him at work on his papers.[23] At about the same time, Thoreau's aunt Louisa asked him if he had made his peace with God. Thoreau replied, "I was never aware we had ever quarreled, Aunt."[24] Though he continually said he had no regrets, he did have one concern: the "Allegash and East Branch" chapter of *The Maine Woods,* which, as he told his old walking companion, William Ellery Channing, was still in a snarl.[25]

On Monday, May 5, 1862, Channing and Alcott called for the last time. Before they left, Alcott leaned over and kissed Thoreau's forehead, "with the damps of death upon it."[26] That night Thoreau asked Sophia to fetch his old friend, the farmer Edmund Hosmer, to sit up with him. As Hosmer was leaving in the morning, Thoreau whispered to Sophia to give the farmer his own copy of *A Week,* the one containing a lock of his brother John's hair.[27] Then Thoreau and Sophia picked up their work where they had left off the day before: she continued reading aloud the section of *A Week*'s "Friday" chapter in which the brothers begin their rapid homeward journey. "Now comes good sailing," he whispered.

A little after seven in the morning, Judge Hoar paid a call, bringing along some fresh hyacinths he had just picked in his garden. Thoreau sniffed them and managed to murmur, "I like them." After the judge left, Thoreau began to exhibit the tell-tale restlessness that precedes death. His mother, Sophia, and Aunt Louisa gathered around him for the familiar vigil. Sometime after eight he asked to be raised up. He spoke a little, mostly unintelligibly, though according to Channing, Sophia thought she could make out the words "moose" and "Indian." Like his father before him, his breathing slowed imperceptibly, but by nine they knew he was gone. He was two months shy of his forty-fifth birthday.

In his funeral elegy, Emerson referred to his friend's "broken task," a theme many of Thoreau's survivors echoed. Yet there were other strains in mourners' reactions to his dying.[28] The most obvious is that, by dying young, Thoreau had generated the widespread interest in his writing he had not enjoyed in his lifetime. News of his death was eagerly disseminated in the eastern press, particularly by James T. Fields, who had been soliciting revisions of Thoreau's essays and papers for posthumous publication in the *Atlantic Monthly* as well as planning posthumous publication and republication of his books. The *New-York Daily Tribune*'s review of "Walking," published in the *Atlantic* on May 28, 1862, was typical of the press's elegiac tone: "The quaint, characteristic essay [is] . . . by the late Henry Thoreau, whose recent decease imports an additional interest to every production of his unique pen."[29]

Moreover, by dying during the early part of the Civil War, Thoreau became a kind of war casualty himself, a martyr to his abolitionist principles as well as to his diseased lungs. In a letter to Ricketson, Sophia spoke of Emerson's funeral elegy: "It is a source of great satisfaction that one so gifted knew and loved my brother and is prepared to speak such brave words about him at this time."[30]

In his journal, Emerson's epithet for Thoreau was frequently "my brave Henry." The etymology of the word *brave* has interesting valence in regard to Thoreau, his death, and the historical context of 1862. According to *The Oxford English Dictionary*, the word means not only "courageous, intrepid, and stout-hearted" but also "worthy, excellent, good." In the minds of his contemporaries, Thoreau's timely yet untimely death resonated with other "brave" lives and deaths—the Union dead, John Brown's execution, the crucifixion of Christ. According to the historian Richard W. Fox, "in the 1840s Thoreau may have been the most radical dissenter on the subject of Jesus in all of America." Yet he also notes how frequently and easily Thoreau availed himself of the Christ imagery of his day.[31] As David S. Reynolds has pointed out, he forthrightly employed the idea of the crucifixion in his depiction of Brown's martyrdom. Fox argues that it took some courage to directly make this link between Brown and Christ; not until the assassination of Lincoln on Good Friday 1865 did pastors and journalists begin to draw such clear parallels between Jesus and an American public figure. Yet both Fox and Reynolds believe that, by the spring of 1862, the combination of Brown's execution and the ubiquity of the Civil War dead made likeness to Jesus an easy association.

A piece by Samuel Ripley Bartlett, which appeared in the *Concord Monitor* on May 17, 1862, illustrates the way in which Thoreau himself was "Christified" after his death. Borrowing the Lord's Supper imagery that Thoreau had used in his own nature essays, Bartlett writes:

> Few at first trod the path to the little house in the wood near Walden. Others now have found the way and the path is a beaten highway. Come, all of you, young and old, boy and girl, man and woman, along the path through the pines. Enter the simple door. Meekly bend your head and gratefully gather around the board he has spread for you. Drink the water he pores from the homely cup. He draws at the fountain of truth. Eat your fill of the bread he has broken and freely offers to all. This house is gone long ago; but still by the shore he loved; the one that is true and pure enough can take the warm hand and feel the throb of the faithful heart of Henry D. Thoreau.[32]

III

In the antebellum period, photography was a growing cottage industry, and photographs became a familiar form of sentimental memorialization. Among the earliest examples were small carrying-case daguerreotypes of young women, often with memento mori verses handwritten on the cases' inner lids. Here is a typical poem from one of these cases:

> This is the likeness of Caroline Christ.
> When I am dead and in my grave
> And when my bones are rotten
> When this you see remember me
> Or I shall be forgotten. The grass is green

The rose is red.
Here is my name when I am dead.
Letherolfsville October 29 AD 1859

Memorializing sentiments and imagery were a part of the culture of Concord. As I noted in a previous chapter, in the summer of 1841, John Thoreau, Jr., convinced five-year-old Waldo Emerson to pose for a traveling daguerreotypist. Because both Waldo and John died during the following January, the photograph became an invaluable memorial of both. In the spring of 1849, when Thoreau's older sister Helen was dying of consumption, Henry (probably with thoughts of John on his mind) had a daguerreotypist come to the family home to make likenesses of both of his sisters. These were the only pictures ever made of them, and Helen died a month later. Sitting for the picture "was a tiring experience . . . in her weakened condition but she was gratified by her brother's thoughtfulness."[33]

Only three likenesses of Thoreau made in his lifetime survive: the 1854 Rowse crayon sketch, the 1856 Maxham daguerreotype, and the 1861 Dunshee ambrotype.[34] As I mentioned previously in the chapter, the Dunshee was made during Thoreau's last visit to Ricketson in New Bedford, nine months before his death. When Sophia wrote to Ricketson to share the details of Henry's death, she asked for a copy. In her letter of thanks she said, "Until a few weeks since, I did not know he had his picture taken in New Bedford last; he accidentally spoke of it, and said you considered it a good likeness." Surely he had known, however, that the picture would eventually arrive to comfort his family. Sophia's letter continues: "I need not tell you, for I cannot, how agreeably surprised I was on opening the little box, to find my own lost brother again. I could not restrain my tears. The picture is invaluable to us."[35]

Thoreau crafted his sentimental reading of himself to the sound of the piano that Sophia, his only surviving sibling, was playing in the parlor. In a series of novelistic repetitions, he returned three times in his Journal, between the fall of 1851 and the spring of 1852, to this scene: he is in his attic room and is being pulled toward the parlor below by the sound of Sophia's piano. On November 11 he tries to be disdainful:

When I have been confined to my chamber for the greater part of several days by some employment or perchance the ague—till I felt weary and house-worn—I have become conscious of a certain softness to which I am otherwise & commonly a stranger—in which the gates were loosened to some emotions—And if I were to become a confirmed invalid I see how sympathy with mankind & society might spring up.[36]

At the time of this writing, Thoreau had nearly another decade left before he would become a confirmed invalid, yet the entry eerily anticipates the reality of his dying, when his frailty finally brought him down to the parlor for good, when he opened himself to the tender ministrations of both his womenfolk and his townspeople.

In the scene in his January 24 Journal entry, he is again in his attic room listening to Sophia at the piano, but this time the music "reminds me of strains which once I heard more frequently—when possessed with the inaudible rhythm I sought my chamber—& communed with my own thoughts. I feel as if then I received the gifts of the gods with too much indifference . . . Now I hear those strains but seldom . . . I cannot dip my pen in it. I cannot work the vein it is so fine & volatile—Ah sweet ineffable reminiscences."[37] Finally, on April 11, he wrote:

> I hear the sound of the piano below as I write this and feel as if the winter in me were at length beginning to thaw—for my spring has been more backwards than nature's. For a month past life has been a thing incredible to me. None but the kind gods can make me sane—If only they will let their south winds blow on me. I ask to be melted. You can only ask of the metals that they be tender to the fire that *melts* them.[38]

There is a room in the Concord Museum devoted to Thoreau's possessions: the furniture he gathered and constructed for his Walden house, including the small bed in which he died; a glass case containing his flute and the pencils he manufactured with his father. At one time the case also held an old wooden pen, its metal tip rusted away almost to nothing. Tied to it still is a strip of paper on which is written in Sophia's faded hand "The last pen brother Henry wrote with." As Thoreau's amanuensis and in many ways his closest companion at the end of his life, his sister was the most significant sentimental reader of his dying and one of the early and important disseminators of the Thoreauvian character into American culture. Sophia drew the original cabin sketch for the cover of *Walden* and ran the family's plumbago business, first with Henry and, after his decline and death, by herself. Thoreau left all his papers to her, including his enormous Journal. With the help of Emerson, Channing, Sanborn, and Blake, she prepared what she could for publication. Before her death in 1876 she willed them to Blake, and after his death, the papers began to scatter.

Shortly after Thoreau's death, the pilgrims began to come to Concord and Walden, often stopping at the Yellow House, where Mrs. Thoreau and Sophia treated them hospitably. Neither woman ever really recovered from Henry's death. Sophia wrote to Ricketson a year later:

> I always reproach myself for any sadness in view of dear Henry's departure, knowing that the possession of such a priceless treasure as he was to us, for so long a time, should ever fill our hearts with gratitude. But I have passed the round of one year with no earthly friend to lean upon—the spring finds us in feeble health . . . I miss so much the counsel of my precious brother, who was never cast down and who in every emergency could make the light shine, that I confess, my heart at times is heavy.[39]

Earlier that year, on February 7 she had written to him:

> You are evidently not aware that I have been recently called to pass through a most fiery trial. Seven weeks ago yesterday, my poor mother fell down our back stairway . . . shattering her right arm frightfully, and otherwise seriously injuring herself. For an hour or two she was deprived of her senses, and during her insanity it was heartrending to me to hear her call almost incessantly for Henry, so sadly did I miss his strong arm and kind, brave heart in that dark hour.[40]

Sophia looked for her brother not only in his literary remains but in the familiar woods and fields around Concord. In this way, she, too, became a Thoreau pilgrim. She wrote to Ricketson on December 15, 1863:

> I spend much time out of doors, visit Walden very often, and the other day I enticed my good aunt Jennie, who will be 79 years old Christmas Day, to accompany me to the pond. It gave her much satisfaction to visit the spot where dear Henry enjoyed so much. I walked up to the north part of the town lately, where his little house now stands [it was being used as a corncrib], and ate my dinner under its roof, with the mice for company.[41]

The members of the Thoreau family, including Henry, were originally buried in the New Burying Ground, located on Bedford Street. When Sleepy Hollow Cemetery was dedicated in the 1850s, Emerson bought a large plot on a shaded hillside. In 1864 Hawthorne was buried on the same hilltop, and soon thereafter the Alcotts bought a neighboring plot. According to the historian W. Barksdale Maynard,

> Within a few years—probably 1866, certainly by 1868—Thoreau's body (along with his family) was moved from the town burying ground to lie near the Hawthorne and Alcott plots, and Authors' Ridge was born,

another destination for the literary pilgrim. To dig the moldering coffins from the ground and cart them to Sleepy Hollow suggests the deliberateness with which Sophia Thoreau managed the memory of her beloved brother and sought to place him prominently before the public eye.[42]

After the death of her voluble and opinionated mother in 1872, Sophia sold the Yellow House, where the family had lived since 1850, to the Alcotts and moved to Maine, where her remaining relatives could care for her in her decline. In 1876 her cousin George Thatcher, who had accompanied Thoreau on two of his Maine excursions, brought Sophia's body home to the family plot in Sleepy Hollow. Years before, after she had moved the family bodies to Authors' Ridge, she had "said, as she looked upon his low head-stone on the hillside, 'Concord is Henry's monument, covered with suitable inscriptions by his own hand.'"[43]

IV

Sophia's version of Thoreau was not everyone's version. In particular, her sentimental reading of him rubbed against Emerson's heroic reading. Though at first she had been pleased with Emerson's eulogy, her opinion changed, especially after the two collaborated on her brother's *Letters to Various Persons.* In a February 2, 1863, letter to Ricketson, she discussed the published version of the eulogy: "You know [Emerson] always eschewed pathos, and reading it for consolation as a stricken mourner, I felt somewhat disappointed. Henry never impressed me as the Stoic Mr. E. represents him. I think Henry was a person of much more faith than Mr. Emerson."[44] This impression was heightened when Emerson assumed the editorship of Thoreau's letters in 1865. She told Ricketson in a July 17, 1965, letter that she was upset to learn that some of her favorite passages of the letters had been omitted, those "betraying natural affection." She confronted Mrs. Emerson about the matter, "who said her husband was a Greek, and treated his own writings in the same manner."[45] Eventually the disputed passages were restored, but Sophia told Ricketson that Emerson had "*bragged* that the coming volume would be a most perfect piece of stoicism, and he feared I had marred his classic stature."[46]

Many Thoreauvians have agreed with Sophia, but I take Emerson's part. Like Richardson, I believe that "'Thoreau' is Emerson's last sustained major piece of writing. A great prose elegy, as good in its way as 'Lycidas,' this is Emerson's best, most personal biographical piece and it remains the best single piece yet written on Henry Thoreau."[47] One can see "Thoreau" as Emerson's final chapter of *Representative Men*. Other chapters of that book describe a philosopher, a skeptic, a writer, a poet and a man of the world, but not until the death of "my brave Henry" (the only American he discussed and the only person he knew personally) did he find a stoic.[48] In each of the men he featured in that collection, Emerson saw reflections of himself as well as major flaws—in Thoreau's case, a lack of ambition. But by emphasizing the stoic in Thoreau, he was able to attend to what he saw as his friend's most distinctive characteristic: heroism.

Emerson's eulogy makes subtle use of antebellum death culture. Although it never directly refers to Thoreau's dying, it twice mentions Thoreau's "holy living," no doubt alluding to Jeremy Taylor's books (which I discussed in a previous chapter) and implying that being "the bachelor of nature" and having "no vices" laid the groundwork for Thoreau's cheerful virtue in dying. The address eulogizes three avatars: Henry, Mr. Thoreau, and Thoreau. Henry is the son, brother, and friend who grew to manhood among the scenes and neighbors of Concord. Intimate and often a contrarian, he "designed superior pencils" and kindly told his friend's teenaged daughter that he hoped his upcoming lecture would please her. "In any circumstance . . . it interested bystanders to know what part he would take . . . and he would not disappoint expectation."[49]

Mr. Thoreau was a writer and a citizen. He used logic to convince the president of Harvard University to give him library privileges. This avatar made "the fields, hills, and waters of his native town . . . known and interesting to all reading Americans and to people over the sea," and gained the respect of his townspeople, who had once castigated his oddities, thanks to his skill in surveying and his encyclopedic knowledge of Concord's land, creatures, and history.[50]

Thoreau was a hero, a prophet, and a "true protestant." He "never faltered," for "there was somewhat military in his nature . . . always manly and able." "No truer American existed."[51] Thoreau was among the first to recognize the iconic stature of John Brown, calling together his townspeople in the vestry of the First Parish Church to share "his earnest eulogy of the hero [which] was heard by all respectfully, by many with a sympathy

that surprised themselves."[52] Alcott had wanted to eulogize Thoreau outdoors, but Emerson had insisted that the funeral be held at this church,
even though Thoreau had "signed off" from it years ago, so that he could
celebrate Thoreau the hero in the same edifice where Thoreau had celebrated Brown the hero.

Emerson's Thoreauvian trinity interweaves but never overlaps. "Mr.
Thoreau" may have acquired the library privileges, but he did so because
"Thoreau, and not the Librarian was the proper custodian" of those pre-
cious books.[53] "Henry" may have badly sprained his ankle in a fall on
Mount Washington, but the fall enabled "Thoreau," the prophet of nature,
to discover a long-sought rare plant.

Nonetheless, two passages have bothered Thoreauvians for generations.
The first begins, "I cannot help counting it a fault in him that he had no
ambition. Wanting this, instead of engineering for all America, he was
captain of a huckleberry party."[54] The second centers around the strange
ending, which compares Thoreau to Tyrolese youths tempted to climb
tall cliffs to gather a flower called "life-everlasting" and "noble purity" for
their beloveds and instead being found "dead at the foot with the flower
in [their] hand[s]."[55] Emerson may have chosen to include the first passage
not only to emphasize common humanity by pointing out a flaw but also
because it worked well in an oral address at a funeral. No doubt it evoked
affectionate chuckles from his auditors: Henry, after all, had spent much
time gathering, talking, and writing about berries. Other passages in the
address bear out this idea that Emerson was speaking to please family and
friends. The "young girl" whom Henry had hoped would enjoy his lecture
was Emerson's own daughter, Edith; the "young man" about to head west
was his son, Edward. Though Thoreau was not a particularly handsome
man, Emerson worked to please his friend's female relatives by referring to
Thoreau's "becoming beard."[56] Such details pleased the audience, as Sophia
indicated in her initial response to the eulogy. However, its comfort did
not translate well to text. Once printed, the remarks lost their immediacy
and seemed less a loving tribute and more a statement of disappointment.

Regarding the second passage, many readers have underestimated the
immense tribute Emerson was paying to Thoreau's heroism, a characteristic that both men had seen as a prime human virtue. The dead young men
clutching "noble purity" and "life-everlasting" are self-referential, and the
anecdote about Thoreau's sprained ankle and the rare plant foreshadows

this conclusion. Emerson understood that Thoreau's perpetual search for rare plants was neither a hobby nor an acknowledged vocation. Rather, the younger man had always seen the heroic in the natural scientist. In 1842, Emerson had asked Thoreau to write an essay titled "Natural History of Massachusetts" for publication in the *Dial*. In that essay, Thoreau had said, "What an admirable training is science for the more active warfare of life." He went on to note that Linnaeus was more brave and heroic than Bonaparte was: "Science is always brave, for to know, is to know good; doubt and danger quail before her eye. What the coward overlooks in his hurry, she calmly scrutinizes, breaking ground like a pioneer for the array of arts that follow in her train. But cowardice is unscientific; for there cannot be a science of ignorance."[57] All his adult life, Thoreau had pursued nature as a holy and heroic quest. Thus, Emerson's reference to dying at the instant of discovering "life-everlasting," the grail of nobility and purity, was an acknowledgment of Thoreau's heroic death.

V

Always, Thoreau looked for past and future seasons in the constant motion of the present season. Natural time has an eternal present, whereas human time is linear: we must eventually die out of nature. Where, then, does a human consciousness go?

In a May 1, 1858, Journal entry, Thoreau wrote of hearing his neighbor's voice at a distance: "I know that this sound was made by the lungs and larynx of E. Wood . . . He can impress himself on the very atmosphere, and then can launch himself a mile on the wind . . . and yet arrive distinct to my ear . . . and yet this creature that is felt so far, that was so noticeable, lives but a short time, quietly dies, and makes no more noise that I know of."[58] This metaphysical conundrum plagued Thoreau throughout his life. During his last winter, he whispered to Channing as they sat by the frost-covered window, "I cannot see on the outside at all. We thought ourselves great philosophers in those wet days when we used to go outside and sit down by these wall-sides."[59] Were they no longer philosophers because they did not sit in the wet? Is there some eternal present where the two philosophers still sit beside those walls, where Elijah Wood's voice still impresses the atmosphere?

The closest Thoreau could come to a solution was his prolonged state of liminality as he was slowly dying. As his physical body wasted away, his consciousness remained; in a sense, he was both alive and dead in a perfect state of transition. And he was in no hurry for this state to end. Unlike his father, who had been impatient to depart once he had taken leave of his family, Thoreau remained interested and amused. He had his family rearrange the furniture in the parlor so he could study the unfamiliar shadows in the night when his illness kept him awake. He told his sister, "Sophia, my knees look like balls on string,—I go on as if I were to stay a thousand years. I do enjoy myself."[60] Some readers have questioned the exultation he felt in his last months, even crediting it to his high fever. But it may have been a direct result of his prolonged experience of the transition from physical to mystical. Beyond change, beyond war, he lingered as mindfully as he had always lived, not the least bit interested in catching a glimpse of the other shore.

While preparing one of his several Thoreau biographies, Sanborn wrote to Parker Pillsbury, an abolitionist minister and Thoreau family friend, requesting details of his last visit with Thoreau. Pillsbury responded:

> He sat pillowed in an easy chair. Behind him stood his patient, dear, devoted mother, with a fan in one hand, and a phial of ammonia or cologne in the other, to sustain him in the warm morning. At the table near him, piled high with his papers and articles related to them and him, sat his sister arranging them, as I understood, for Ticknor and Fields, who had been to Concord and bought the copyright. When I entered Thoreau was looking deathly weak and pale. I saw my way for but the fewest words. I said, as I took his hand, "I suppose this is the best you can do now." He smiled and only nodded, and gasped a faint assent. "The outworks," I said, "seem almost ready to give way." Then a smile shone on his pale face and with an effort he said, "Yes,—but as long as she cracks she holds" (a common saying of boys skating).[61] Then I spoke only once more to him, and I cannot remember my exact words. But I think my question was substantially this: "You seem so near the dark river, that I almost wonder how the opposite shore may appear to you." Then he answered: "One world at a time."[62]

The phrase "one world at a time" may be more famous as dying words, but "as long as she cracks she holds" is an extraordinarily nuanced response. I read it as another way of saying "one world at a time," using provincial language to locate himself in a specific time and place. By expressing the sentiment twice, Thoreau is emphasizing that, despite his frail and fading frame, his consciousness remains firmly with the woods, waters, and meadows of Concord. As long as winter holds, spring, in the form of the ice breakup, is kept at bay. Winter dies so that spring can be born, but Thoreau is not yet ready to die out of nature. The bluebirds may have returned, the judge is picking hyacinths in his garden, but Pillsbury and all of us must wait on nature's good time for winter to go about its dying.

Notes

Introduction. Anticipation as Prophecy

Epigraph: Henry David Thoreau, *A Week on the Concord and Merrimack Rivers, Walden, The Maine Woods, Cape Cod,* ed. Robert F. Sayre (New York: Library of America, 1985), 583. Subsequent citations from this volume refer to the specific titles of each work.

1. Thoreau, *Walden,* 400.
2. Philippe Ariès, *The Hour of Our Death,* trans. Helen Weaver (New York: Vintage, 1982), 409.
3. Jeremy Taylor, *The Rule and Exercise of Holy Dying* (Cambridge: Dutton, 1876); Jeremy Taylor, *The Rule and Exercise of Holy Living* (Cambridge: Dutton, 1828).
4. Lidian Jackson Emerson, *Selected Letters of Lidian Jackson Emerson,* ed. Delores Bird Carpenter (Columbia: University of Missouri Press, 1987), 99, 100.
5. Anna Ricketson and Walton Ricketson, eds., *Daniel Ricketson and His Friends* (Boston: Houghton Mifflin, 1902), 141.
6. Lewis O. Saum, "Death in Pre–Civil War America," in *Death in America,* ed. David E. Stannard (Philadelphia: University of Pennsylvania Press, 1977), 41.
7. Ibid., 48.
8. Joanne Dobson, "Reclaiming Sentimental Literature," *American Literature* 69 (June 1997): 267.
9. Thoreau, *Walden,* 327.
10. Henry David Thoreau, *Journal,* vol. 1, *1837–1844,* ed. Elizabeth Hall Witherell, William L. Howarth, Robert Sattlemayer, and Thomas Blanding, in *The Writings of Henry David Thoreau,* ser. ed. Elizabeth Hall Witherell (Princeton: Princeton University Press, 1981), 372.
11. Ralph Waldo Emerson, *Emerson in His Journals,* ed. Joel Porte (Cambridge: Harvard University Press, 1982), 511.
12. Ralph Waldo Emerson, "Self-Reliance," in *Essays and Lectures,* ed. Joel Porte (New York: Library of America, 1983), 271.
13. Thoreau, *Walden,* 336.
14. Ralph Waldo Emerson, "Experience," in *Essays and Lectures,* 480.
15. Henry David Thoreau, *Collected Essays and Poems,* ed. Elizabeth Hall Witherell (New York: Library of America, 2001), 231–33.
16. Thoreau, *Walden,* 394.
17. My thanks to Robert Gross for sharing biographical information about Wood and Dugan.
18. Thoreau, *A Week,* 368.

19. Thoreau, *Essays and Poems*, 233.

20. Henry David Thoreau, *The Journals of Henry D. Thoreau: In Fourteen Volumes Bound as Two* (1906; New York: Dover, 1962), 2:348–49.

21. Randal Conrad, "An Infinite Road to the Golden Age: A Close Reading of Thoreau's 'Road—That old Carlisle One' in the Late Journal," in *Thoreauvian Modernities: Transatlantic Conversations of an American Icon,* ed. Francois Secq, Laura Dassow Walls, and Michael Granger (Athens: University of Georgia Press, 2013), 86, 89.

22. Ibid., 84–85.

23. According to Alan D. Hodder, the three Thoreaus were created first by the market and then by the act of literary canonization (*Thoreau's Ecstatic Witness* [New Haven: Yale University Press, 2001]). Thoreau's immediate survivors promoted him as a gentle nature writer to preserve and increase his burgeoning literary reputation. His friend Harrison Blake was the first to publish the Journal, which he released as seasonal excerpts. Toward the end of the nineteenth century, however, British Socialists began identifying with Thoreau as a brother activist. The fame of this new political Thoreau quickly spread, and both Mahatma Gandhi and Martin Luther King, Jr., eventually attached themselves to this version of the writer. In 1941, with the publication of F. O. Matthiessen's *American Renaissance,* Thoreau's reputation as a brilliant stylist was established.

24. Lawrence Buell, *The Environmental Imagination: Thoreau, Nature Writing, and the Formation of American Culture* (Cambridge: Belknap, 1995); Laura Dassow Walls, *Seeing New Worlds: Henry David Thoreau and Nineteenth-Century Natural Science* (Madison: University of Wisconsin Press, 1995).

25. David S. Reynolds, *John Brown, Abolitionist: The Man Who Killed Slavery, Sparked the Civil War, and Seeded Civil Rights* (New York: Knopf, 2005).

26. Sherman Paul, *The Shores of America: Thoreau's Inward Exploration* (Urbana: University of Chicago Press, 1958).

27. Thoreau, *Essays and Poems,* 442.

28. Ralph Waldo Emerson, "History," in *Essays and Lectures,* 237.

29. Robert D. Richardson, *Henry Thoreau: A Life of the Mind* (Berkeley: University of California Press, 1986), 385.

30. An example of this use of *realize* appears in the story of the aging and heavyset Elizabeth Peabody, transcendentalist writer, editor, educator, and conversationalist, who fell on her back after walking into a tree. Cushioned by her voluminous skirts, she was unhurt. As her nieces and nephews hauled her to her feet, they asked her why she hadn't seen the tree. "I saw it," she is supposed to have said, "but I had not realized it" (Bruce A. Ronda, *Elizabeth Peabody: A Reformer on Her Own Terms* [Cambridge: Harvard University Press, 1999], 261).

31. Krista Tippett writes, "Before Newton and Galileo, ancient cultures thought of time as organic, subjective, cyclical, and part of nature. Only in the nineteenth century did science and industry teach society to think of time as a matter of fixed precision. The railroads were being established and it was important for people to be at the station on time" (*Speaking of Faith: Why Religion Matters—and How to Talk about It* [New York: Penguin, 2008], 103).

32. Thoreau, *Walden,* 520, 336; Psalm 119:147–50, King James Version.

33. According to the translator Robert Alter, "the Hebrew verb, *quidem,* here, . . . can equally mean 'to anticipate,' 'to go before.' " In Psalm 119, the King James version renders *quidem* "as 'prevent,' using the English verb with precisely the same meaning, which is now obsolete. [It] present[s] us, in reverse chronological order, the picture of a supplicant who spends the whole night in a prayer vigil that lasts till daybreak" (*The Book of Psalms* [New York: Norton, 2008], 431–32, n. 147).

34. Thoreau, *Walden,* 336.

35. Ibid.
36. Thoreau's mother's family descended from the early Puritans, but his father's ancestors emigrated from the island of Jersey a few years before the American Revolution.
37. Douglas B. Smith, *Ever Wonder Why?* (New York: Ballantine, 2013), 111.
38. William Woys Weaver, *America Eats: Forms of Edible Folk Art* (New York: Harper and Row, 1989), 108.
39. Thoreau, *Walden*, 581.
40. Thoreau, *Essays and Poems*, 357–58.
41. Thoreau, *Walden*, 581–82.
42. Ibid., 576. Thoreau may have connected the Greek idea of *kairos* to his understanding of anticipation as prophecy. *The Oxford English Dictionary* defines *kairos* as "the propitious moment for the performance of an action or the coming into being of a new state."
43. Richardson, *Henry Thoreau*, 206.
44. *The Bhagavad Gita*, trans. Eknath Easwaran (Tomales, Calif.: Nilgiri, 2007), 89.
45. Thoreau, *Walden*, 582–83.
46. Hodder, *Thoreau's Ecstatic Witness*, 209–10.
47. *Bhagavad Gita*, 165–66.
48. Walter Harding, *The Days of Henry Thoreau: A Biography* (New York: Dover, 1982), 466.
49. *Bhagavad Gita*, 168.
50. Thoreau, *Essays and Poems*, 253.
51. Thoreau, *Walden*, 587.
52. Ibid., 580.
53. Ibid., 453.
54. Ibid., 563.
55. Ibid., 355, 390 Caged songbirds were common pets for women in the antebellum period, and boys often captured wild songbirds to sell. As both the pet industry and the eastern forests became more developed, imported tropical birds became more popular (Katherine C. Grier, *Pets in America: A History* [Chapel Hill: University of North Carolina Press, 2006]). Though I doubt the Thoreau women would have kept caged birds, they were common in the town. Emerson's daughter had a canary, and his wife had a parrot that on at least one occasion caused considerable pandemonium.
56. Thoreau, *Walden*, 571.
57. Ibid., 572. It is a testament to the wonderful care of Thoreau's prose that this solitary goose is seeking not a mate but a "companion," the friend that Thoreau cannot find.
58. Ibid., 574.
59. Ibid., 511.

1. Figure in the Mist

Epigraph: Annie Russell Marble, *Thoreau: His Home, Friends, and Books* (New York: Crowell, 1902), 52.

1. Henry David Thoreau, *A Week on the Concord and Merrimack Rivers, Walden, The Maine Woods, Cape Cod,* ed. Robert F. Sayre (New York: Library of America, 1985). Subsequent citations from this volume refer to the specific titles of each work.
2. Robert D. Richardson, Jr., *Henry Thoreau: A Life of the Mind* (Berkeley: University of California Press, 1986), 113.
3. Ibid., 117.
4. Ralph Waldo Emerson, *The Letters of Ralph Waldo Emerson in Six Volumes,* ed. Ralph L. Rusk (New York: New York University Press, 1939), 3:4.

5. Richardson, *Henry Thoreau*, 117.

6. Scarlet fever was also known as scarlatina. Before the days of antibiotics, it could quickly kill a previously healthy child.

7. Ralph Waldo Emerson, *Emerson in His Journal*, ed. Joel Porte (Cambridge: Harvard University Press, 1982), 497.

8. Henry I. Bowditch, *Consumption in New England: Locality as One of Its Chief Causes. An Address Delivered before the Massachusetts Medical Society* (Boston: Ticknor and Fields, 1862), vi.

9. Evelyn Barish, "The Moonless Night: Emerson's Crisis of Health, 1825–1827," in *Emerson Centenary Essays*, ed. Joel Myerson (Carbondale: Southern Illinois University Press, 1982), 9.

10. Marble, *Thoreau*, 35.

11. Robert D. Richardson, Jr., *Emerson: The Mind on Fire* (Berkeley: University of California Press, 1995), 120.

12. Edward Waldo Emerson, *Henry David Thoreau as Remembered by a Young Friend* (1917; reprint, New York: Dover, 1999), 49.

13. Richardson, *Emerson*, 91–92.

14. The transcendentalists (who did not give themselves this name) called their philosophy "the newness," or, as Emerson succinctly put it, "idealism as it appears in 1842" (Ralph Waldo Emerson, "The Transcendentalist," in *Essays and Lectures*, ed. Joel Porte [New York: Library of America, 1983], 193).

15. Henry David Thoreau, *The Correspondence of Henry David Thoreau*, ed. Walter Harding and Carl Bode (New York: New York University Press, 1958), 15–18.

16. Henry David Thoreau, *Collected Essays and Poems*, ed. Elizabeth Hall Witherell (New York: Library of America, 2001), 524–25.

17. Richardson, *Henry Thoreau*, 58.

18. Thoreau, *Essays and Poems*, 524–25.

19. Thoreau, *A Week*, 99.

20. Richardson, *Henry Thoreau*, 61–62.

21. Thoreau, *A Week*, 38, 35.

22. Ibid., 13.

23. Ibid., 48.

24. Ibid., 71.

25. Ibid., 49.

26. Henry David Thoreau, *The Maine Woods*, 645.

27. Thoreau, *A Week*, 99, 103.

28. Ibid., 125.

29. Ibid., 131.

30. Ibid., 180–81.

31. Ibid., 159.

32. Ibid., 94.

33. Ibid., 152.

34. Ibid., 153, 155.

35. Ibid., 177.

36. Ibid., 202.

37. Ibid., 201–202.

38. Laura Dassow Walls, "Walking West, Gazing East: Planetarity on the Shores of Cape Cod," in *Thoreauvian Modernities: Transatlantic Conversations on an American Icon*, ed. Francois Specq, Laura Dassow Walls, and Michael Granger (Athens: University of Georgia Press, 2013), 26.

39. Thoreau, *A Week*, 204, 216.

40. Ibid., 217, 219.

41. Ibid., 224.
42. Ibid., 226.
43. Ibid., 232.
44. Ibid., 233.
45. Thoreau, *Walden,* 336.
46. Ibid., 242.
47. Ibid., 246.
48. Ibid., 246–47.
49. Ibid., 247.
50. Ibid., 258.
51. Ibid., 261.
52. Ibid., 250.
53. H. Daniel Peck, *Thoreau's Morning Work: Memory and Perception in "A Week on the Concord and Merrimack Rivers," the Journal, and "Walden"* (New Haven: Yale University Press, 1990), 19–20.
54. Thoreau, *A Week,* 263.
55. Ibid., 264.
56. Ibid.
57. Steven Fink, *Prophet in the Marketplace: Thoreau's Development as a Professional Writer* (Princeton: Princeton University Press, 1992), 227.
58. Thoreau, *A Week,* 265.
59. Ibid., 43.
60. Ibid., 21–22.
61. Ibid., 290.
62. Ibid., 268.
63. *The Bhagavad Gita,* trans. Eknath Easwaran (Tomales, Calif.: Nilgiri, 2007), 89.
64. Robert Milder, *Reimagining Thoreau* (Cambridge: Cambridge University Press), 43.
65. Ibid., 293.
66. Thoreau, *A Week,* 292.
67. Ibid., 270.
68. Ibid., 272.
69. Ibid., 273.
70. Ibid., 277.
71. Ibid., 279.
72. Ibid., 287.
73. Ibid., 287.
74. Ibid., 307.
75. Ibid.
76. Ibid., 315.
77. Ibid., 272–73.
78. Ibid., 273.
79. Ibid., 287.
80. Ibid., 286.
81. Thoreau, *Walden,* 574.
82. Thoreau, *A Week,* 316.
83. Ibid., 316–17.
84. Ibid., 317.
85. Henry David Thoreau, *Journal,* vol. 1, *1837–1844,* ed. Elizabeth Hall Witherell, William L. Howarth, Robert Sattlemayer, and Thomas Blanding, in *The Writings of Henry David Thoreau,* ser. ed. Elizabeth Hall Witherell (Princeton: Princeton University Press, 1981), 350.

86. Thoreau, *A Week,* 319.

87. Ibid.

2. "I did not cry"

Epigraph: Henry David Thoreau, *Journal,* vol. 4, *1851–1852,* ed. Leonard N. Neufeldt and Nancy Craig Simmons, in *The Writings of Henry David Thoreau,* ser. ed. Elizabeth Hall Witherell (Princeton: Princeton University Press, 1992), 18.

1. Henry David Thoreau, *A Week on the Concord and Merrimack Rivers, Walden, The Maine Woods, Cape Cod,* ed. Robert F. Sayre (New York: Library of America, 1985). Subsequent citations from this volume refer to the specific titles of each work.

2. Joanne Dobson, "Reclaiming Sentimental Literature," *American Literature* 69, no. 2 (1997): 265.

3. Ibid., 266.

4. Ibid., 279.

5. Mary Hosmer Brown, *Memories of Concord* (Boston: Four Seasons, 1926), 108.

6. Thoreau, *A Week,* n.p.

7. Henry David Thoreau, *Journal,* vol. 3, *1848–1851,* ed. Robert Sattelmeyer, Mark R. Patterson, and William Rossi, in *The Writings of Henry David Thoreau,* ser. ed. Elizabeth Hall Witherell (Princeton: Princeton University Press, 1991), 68.

8. Henry David Thoreau, *Journal,* vol. 7, *1853–1854,* ed. Nancy Craig Simmons and Ron Thomas, in *The Writings of Henry David Thoreau,* ser. ed. Elizabeth Hall Witherell (Princeton: Princeton University Press, 2009), 189.

9. Thoreau, *The Maine Woods,* 685. Worried about the sacrilegious overtones in "Chesuncook," James Russell Lowell, the editor of the *Atlantic Monthly,* published the essay without the line in which the pine tree goes to heaven. Thoreau was so angry that he never sent another piece to the magazine until Lowell was no longer editor. Even then, he stipulated that he must approve any changes in the manuscript.

10. Elizabeth Stuart Phelps, *The Gates Ajar,* ed. Helen Sootin Smith (Cambridge: Harvard University Press, 1964); George Wood, *The Gates Wide Open; or Scenes from Another World* (Boston: Lee and Shepard, 1869).

11. Thoreau, *Walden,* 549.

12. Thoreau, *A Week,* 180–81.

13. Thoreau, *Walden,* 473.

14. Ibid., 446.

15. Hilderic Friend, *Flowers and Flower-Lore* (London: Swan Sonnenschein, 1884), 52.

16. Henry David Thoreau, *Collected Essays and Poems,* ed. Elizabeth Hall Witherell (New York: Library of America, 2001), 491.

17. Walter Harding, *The Days of Henry Thoreau: A Biography* (New York: Dover, 1962), 11–12.

18. Thoreau, *Journal,* 3:84.

19. Ibid., 3:75.

20. Ibid.

21. Robert D. Richardson, Jr., *Henry Thoreau: A Life of the Mind* (Berkeley: University of California Press, 1986), 389.

22. Vincent J. Bertolini, "Fireside Chastity: The Erotics of Sentimental Bachelorhood in the 1850s," in *Sentimental Men: Masculinity and the Politics of Affect in American Culture,* ed. Mary Chapman and Glenn Hendler (Berkeley: University of California Press, 1999), 32.

23. Henry David Thoreau, letter to Ralph Waldo Emerson, November 14, 1847, and Ralph Waldo Emerson, letter to Henry David Thoreau, December 2, 1847, both in *The*

Correspondence of Henry David Thoreau, ed. Walter Harding and Carl Bode (New York: New York University Press, 1958), 189–95.

24. Ralph Waldo Emerson, *Emerson in His Journals,* ed. Joel Porte (Cambridge: Harvard University Press, 1982), 207; Ralph Waldo Emerson, "Thoreau," in *Emerson: Essays and Poems,* ed. Joel Porte, Harold Bloom, and Paul Kane (New York: Library of America, 1983), 1010.

25. Vincent J. Bertolini, "Fireside Chastity: The Erotics of Sentimental Bachelorhood in the 1850s," in *Sentimental Men: Masculinity and the Politics of Affect in American Culture,* ed. Mary Chapman and Glenn Hendler (Berkeley: University of California Press, 1999), 27.

26. Russ Castronovo, *Necro Citizenship: Death, Eroticism, and the Public Sphere in the Nineteenth–Century United States* (Durham, N.C.: Duke University Press, 2001), 67.

27. Thoreau, *Walden,* 513.

28. Chapman and Hendler, *Sentimental Men,* 9.

29. Thoreau, *Walden,* 513.

30. Ibid., 526.

31. Elise Lemire, *Black Walden: Slavery and Its Aftermath in Concord, Massachusetts* (Philadelphia: University of Pennsylvania Press, 2009), 10–11.

32. Thoreau, *Walden,* 527.

33. Lemire, *Black Walden,* 156.

34. Ibid., 137.

35. Thoreau, *Walden,* 527.

36. Lemire, *Black Walden,* 12.

37. Thoreau, *Walden,* 527.

38. Lemire clarifies, "In fact, it is Sippio Brister . . . who is buried off to the side of the Lincoln cemetery . . . Brister Freeman's burial site is neither marked nor known . . . In insisting that Concord not treat him as a 'foreigner,' Brister should be counted among Concord's great revolutionaries . . . It may be that Henry did not mistake Sippio Brister for Brister Freeman, but rather purposefully conflated them in *Walden* in order to associate the heroic traits of Scipio Africanus with Brister Freeman" (*Black Walden,* 170).

39. Thoreau, *Walden,* 527.

40. Lemire, *Black Walden,* 141.

41. Ibid., 162–63.

42. Thoreau, *Walden,* 528.

43. Ibid., 530.

44. Lemire, *Black Walden,* 163.

45. Thoreau, *Walden,* 530–31.

46. Ibid., 532.

47. Ibid.

48. David F. Wood, *An Observant Eye: The Thoreau Collection at the Concord Museum* (Concord, Mass.: Concord Museum, 2006), 9.

49. Harriet Beecher Stowe, *Uncle Tom's Cabin, The Minister's Wooing, Oldtown Folks,* ed. Kathryn Kish Skylar (New York: Library of America, 1982), 943–44. Subsequent citations from this volume refer to the specific titles of each work.

50. Stowe, *Oldtown Folks,* 1345–46. I do not know if Stowe read Thoreau's writings. However, her husband, Calvin Stowe, owned first editions of *A Week, Cape Cod,* and *The Maine Woods* (which describes in painful detail the "death" of a white pine cut down by loggers). He passed on these books to his son, Lyman, and they were eventually donated to the Concord Antiquarian Society, now the Concord Museum.

51. For the rest of his life, he continued to gather deadfall and driftwood and to dig out old stumps for his family's winter fuel.

52. Thoreau, *Walden,* 524. Although his relationship with Emerson had begun to sour, I don't think that Thoreau is merely talking about deeds and property rights but emphasizing that no one person, by possession or location, truly owns the land.

53. Ibid., 514.

54. Ibid., 523.

55. Anonymous, "The Wood-Fire," in *The Dial: A Magazine for Literature, Philosophy, and Religion* (Boston: Weeks, Jodron, 1840), 1:193. Though Thoreau did not name the poet in the printed text, he took to writing "Mrs. Hooper" next to the poem when he gave out copies of *Walden.* As far as I know, this is the only place where he quotes a woman writer.

56. Thoreau, *Walden,* 525.

57. Fair Haven Bay is a small lake on the Sudbury River, about a mile southwest of Walden.

58. Harding, *Days,* 160.

59. Thoreau, *Journal,* 3:75–80.

60. Thoreau, *Walden,* 523.

61. F. W. Shelton, "On Old Bachelors," *Southern Literary Messenger* 19 (April 1852): 223–28.

62. Ibid., 223.

63. Edward Waldo Emerson, *Henry Thoreau as Remembered by a Young Friend* (1917; reprint, Mineola, N.Y.: Dover, 1999), xii, 2.

64. Thoreau, *Walden,* 351.

65. Ibid., 432–33.

66. Thoreau, *Journal,* 3:n.p.

67. Harding, *Days,* 408.

68. Henry David Thoreau, *Journal,* vol. 5, *1852–1853,* ed. Patrick F. O'Connell, in *The Writings of Henry David Thoreau,* ser. ed. Elizabeth Hall Witherell (Princeton: Princeton University Press, 1995), 150.

69. Jürgen Kloss, "The Adventurous Story of Poor 'Mary of the Wild Moor," *Just Another Tune: Songs and Their History,* http://justanothertune.com.

70. Thoreau, *Walden,* 569–70.

71. Ibid., 503.

72. Ibid., 504.

73. Thoreau, *Journal,* 4:62–63; William Cullen Bryant, "Thanatopsis," in *The Heath Anthology of American Literature,* vol. B, *Early Nineteenth-Century (1800–1865),* ed. Paul Lauter (Belmont, Calif.: Wadsworth Cengage, 2009), 2957–59.

74. Thoreau, *Journal,* 4:225.

3. Blood and Seeds

Epigraphs: Henry David Thoreau, *Journals, 1854,* ed. Sandra Harbert Petrulionis, in *The Writings of Henry David Thoreau,* ser. ed. Elizabeth Hall Witherell (Princeton: Princeton University Press, 2002), 37; and Henry David Thoreau, *The Journal of Henry David Thoreau in Fourteen Volumes Bound as Two,* ed. Bradford Torrey and Francis H. Allen (1906; reprint, New York: Dover, 2002).

1. Thomas Carlyle, *Heroes, Hero Worship, and the Heroic in History* (1841; reprint, New York: Burt, 1947); Henry David Thoreau, *Collected Essays and Poems,* ed. Elizabeth Hall Witherell (New York: Library of America, 2001), 57–88.

2. David S. Reynolds, *John Brown, Abolitionist: The Man Who Killed Slavery, Sparked the Civil War, and Seeded Civil Rights* (New York: Knopf, 2005), 19.

3. Thoreau, *Essays and Poems,* 57.

4. Ibid., 60, 58.

5. Interestingly, although Thoreau mentions Raleigh's famous poem "The Soul's Errand"

in this essay, he doesn't quote it. Some years later, however, he quotes it in full in "The Martyrdom of John Brown."

6. Thoreau, *Essays and Poems,* 69.
7. Ibid., 71.
8. Carlyle, *Heroes,* 41.
9. Reynolds, *John Brown, Abolitionist,* 164.
10. Carlyle, *Heroes,* 269.
11. Robert F. Sayre, *Thoreau and the American Indians* (Princeton: Princeton University Press, 1977), 27.
12. Ibid., 6.
13. Thoreau, *Essays and Poems,* 233.
14. Ibid., 246, 242.
15. Ibid., 374, 375.
16. Ibid., 454.
17. Ibid., 468.
18. Ibid., 402.
19. Ibid., 418.
20. Ibid., 442.
21. Ibid., 370, 371, 373.
22. Ibid., 462.
23. Ibid., 486.
24. Ibid., 383, 402, 404, 414.
25. Ibid., 418–19.
26. Ibid., 434.
27. Ibid., 229.
28. Ibid., 226.
29. Thoreau, *Walden,* 351.
30. Robert D. Richardson, Jr., *Henry Thoreau: A Life of the Mind* (Berkeley: University of California Press, 1986), 257.
31. Thoreau, *Essays and Poems,* 230.
32. Ibid., 226.
33. Ibid., 238–39.
34. Ibid., 239.
35. Ibid., 249.
36. Ibid., 240.
37. Ibid., 248.
38. Ibid., 252.
39. Ibid., 253.
40. Ibid., 229.
41. Ibid., 254.
42. Ibid.
43. Ibid.
44. Ibid., 255.
45. Ibid., 254.
46. Ibid., 255.
47. Ibid., 450.
48. Ibid., 452.
49. Ralph Waldo Emerson, "Thoreau," in *Essays and Poems,* eds. Joel Porte, Harold Bloom, and Paul Kane (New York: Library of America, 1996), 1021.
50. Thoreau, *The Maine Woods,* 713–822.
51. Walter Harding, *The Days of Henry Thoreau* (New York: Dover, 1961), 449. Harding is mistaken about the snowshoes, which Thoreau purchased on one of his trips to Maine

(David F. Wood, *An Observant Eye: The Thoreau Collection at the Concord Museum* [Concord Museum: Concord, Massachusetts, 2006], 54).

52. Corinne Hosfield Smith, *Westward I Go Free: Tracing Thoreau's Last Journey* (Winnipeg: Green Frigate, 2012), 253.

53. John J. Kucich, "Lost in the Maine Woods: Henry David Thoreau, Joseph Nicolar, and the Penobscot World," *Concord Saunterer*, new ser., 19/20 (2011–12): 23.

54. Smith, *Westward*, 263.

55. Ibid., 264.

56. Ibid.

57. Ibid.

58. Ibid., 266. According to the website of the Concord Museum (which now owns the three buckskin garments) only the shirt and dress were made by the Dakota. The trousers were from either the Red River Metis or the Plains Cree tribe. Most likely the Dakota acquired them through trade, but Thoreau may have had an unrecorded encounter with another tribe.

59. Richardson, *Henry Thoreau*, 386.

60. Thoreau, *Essays and Poems*, 452–53.

61. Ironically, the crabapple, which Thoreau believed was wild, had been "transplanted and carefully preserved by the nurseryman Jonathan T. Grimes" (Sayre, *Indians*, 198).

62. Thoreau, *Essays and Poems*, 444.

63. Ibid., 448.

64. Ibid.

65. Ibid., 467.

66. Ronald Wesley Hoag, "Thoreau's Later Natural History Writings," in *The Cambridge Companion to Henry David Thoreau*, ed. Joel Myerson (Cambridge: Cambridge University Press, 1999), 159.

67. Thoreau, *Essays and Poems*, 466.

68. Ibid., 463.

69. Luke 22:19, King James Version.

70. Thoreau, *Essays and Poems*, 466.

71. Ibid., 446.

72. Thoreau, *Walden*, 580.

73. Thoreau, *Essays and Poems*, 455.

74. Ibid., 469.

75. Thoreau was prescient. At the time of this writing, I have never tasted a huckleberry in its wild state. The closest I've come is purchasing huckleberry jam from the Thoreau Society Shop at Walden Pond.

76. Thoreau, *Essays and Poems*, 471.

77. Ibid.

78. Ibid., 475.

79. Thoreau, *Walden*, 487.

80. Thoreau, *Essays and Poems*, 219.

81. Thoreau, *Walden*, 451.

82. Thoreau, *Essays and Poems*, 468.

83. Ibid., 483. Ironically, the Dakota chief Little Crow, whom Thoreau had admired in Minnesota, was killed by an American settler for a bounty not long after Thoreau's death—shot in the back while he gathered berries with his son (Smith, *Westward*, 273.)

84. Thoreau, *Essays and Poems*, 485.

85. Ibid., 491.

86. Ibid., 488.

87. Ibid., 492.

88. Ibid.

89. Ibid., 493.

90. Ibid., 373.

91. Ibid., 374.

92. William Rossi, "Thoreau's Multiple Modernities," in *Thoreauvian Modernities: Transatlantic Conversations on an American Icon,* ed. Francois Specq, Laura Dassow Walls, and Michael Granger (Athens: University of Georgia Press, 2013), 64.

93. Thoreau, *Essays and Poems,* 374, 390.

94. Ibid., 386.

95. Ibid., 378.

96. Ibid., 381.

97. Homer, *Iliad,* trans. Robert Fagles (New York: Penguin, 1991), 605.

98. Thoreau, *Essays and Poems,* 383.

99. In early December 1860, while outside counting tree rings, Thoreau caught a chill that may have brought on his final illness. Some biographers, such as Richardson, believe his fatal decline began when Bronson Alcott, who was suffering from bronchitis, came to discuss a one-year-anniversary memorial for John Brown. If this story were true, then one might say that Thoreau was another casualty of Brown's raid. However, both he and his family believed that the chill was at fault (Harding, *The Days of Henry Thoreau,* 441; Richardson, *Henry Thoreau,* 385).

100. Virgil, *Aeneid,* trans. Robert Fitzgerald (New York: Vintage, 1983), 170.

101. Thoreau, *Essays and Poems,* 380.

102. Ibid., 382.

103. Ibid., 387.

104. Ibid., 387–88.

105. Ibid., 392.

106. Ibid., 253.

107. Ibid., 393.

108. Ibid., 395.

109. Ibid. 387–88.

110. Philip Cafaro, *Thoreau's Living Ethics: "Walden" and the Pursuit of Virtue* (Athens: University of Georgia Press, 2006), 188–89.

111. Thoreau, *Essays and Poems,* 394.

112. Ibid., 404.

113. Ibid., 383.

114. Ibid., 416.

115. Ibid.

116. Ibid.

117. Reynolds, *John Brown, Abolitionist,* 432.

118. Thoreau, *Essays and Poems,* 414.

119. Ibid., 420.

120. Ibid., 422.

121. Ibid., 428.

122. Thoreau *Journal,* ed. Torrey and Allen, 2:400–458.

123. Thoreau, *Essays and Poems,* 428.

124. Ibid., 428.

125. Henry David Thoreau, letter to Franklin Sanborn, June 25, 1861, in *The Correspondence of Henry David Thoreau,* ed. Walter Harding and Carl Bode (New York: New York University Press, 1958), 618–19.

126. Henry David Thoreau, letter to Myron Benton, March 12, 1862, in ibid., 641.

127. Daniel Ricketson, letter to Henry David Thoreau, March 30, 1862, in *Daniel Ricketson and His Friends,* ed. Anna Ricketson and Walton Ricketson (Boston: Houghton Mifflin, 1902), 644.

128. The manuscript is now available under the title *Faith in a Seed,* ed. Bradley P. Dean (Washington, D.C.: Island Press, 1993).

129. Laura Dassow Walls, *Seeing New Worlds: Henry David Thoreau and Nineteenth Century Natural Science* (Madison: University of Wisconsin Press, 1995), 200.

130. Kristen Case, "Thoreau's Radical Empiricism: The Kalendar, Pragmatism, and Science," in Specq et al., *Thoreauvian Modernities,* 187.

131. Thoreau, *Essays and Poems,* 429, 396.

132. Walls, *Seeing New Worlds,* 203.

133. Thoreau, *Essays and Poems,* 430.

134. Ibid.

135. Ibid., 431.

136. Ibid., 436.

137. Ibid., 434.

138. Ibid., 435.

139. Ibid., 436.

140. Ibid., 431.

141. Ibid., 438.

142. Ibid., 439.

143. Ibid., 442.

144. Ibid.

145. Case, "Thoreau's Radical Empiricism," 196.

146. Thoreau, *Essays and Poems,* 443.

147. Dante, *Paradiso,* trans. John D. Sinclair (London: Bodley Head, 1948), 485.

148. Thoreau, *Walden,* 587.

149. Thoreau, *Essays and Poems,* 388.

150. Ibid., 455.

151. Henry David Thoreau, *Journal,* vol. 3, *1848–1851,* ed. Robert Sattelmeyer, Mark R. Patterson, and William Rossi, in *The Writings of Henry David Thoreau,* ser. ed. Elizabeth Hall Witherell (Princeton: Princeton University Press, 1991), 260.

152. Thoreau, *Essays and Poems,* 255.

153. Ibid., 253.

154. Dante Alighieri, *Paradiso,* trans. John D. Sinclair (London: Bodley Head, 1948), 485; Thoreau, *Walden,* 587; Thoreau, *Essays and Poems,* 388, 455; Thoreau, *Journal,* 3:260; Thoreau, *Essays and Poems,* 255, 253, 428.

4. *Artoosoqu'* and the Button

Epigraphs: Henry David Thoreau, *Journal,* vol. 6, *1853,* ed. Robert Sattelmeyer, William Rossi, and Heather Kirk Thomas, in *The Writings of Henry David Thoreau,* ser. ed. Elizabeth Hall Witherell (Princeton: Princeton University Press, 2000), 33; and Henry David Thoreau, *Journal,* vol. 7, *1853–1854,* ed. Nancy Craig Simmons and Ron Thomas, in *The Writings of Henry David Thoreau,* ser. ed. Elizabeth Hall Witherell (Princeton: Princeton University Press, 2009), 243.

1. Henry David Thoreau, *A Week on the Concord and Merrimack Rivers, Walden, The Maine Woods, Cape Cod,* ed. Robert F. Sayre (New York: Library of America, 1985), 400, 565–68. Subsequent citations from this volume refer to the specific titles of each work.

2. Laura Dassow Walls, "Walking West, Gazing East: Planetarity on the Shores of Cape Cod," in *Thoreauvian Modernities: Transatlantic Conversations on an American Icon,* ed. Francois Specq, Laura Dassow Walls, and Michael Granger (Athens: University of Georgia Press, 2013), 24.

3. Thoreau, *Walden*, 523.

4. Ibid., 400.

5. Here Thoreau is using Emerson's concept of *the Me* and *the Not Me*, which Emerson himself had gleaned from Carlyle: "Philosophically considered, the universe is composed of Nature and the Soul. Strictly speaking, therefore, all that is separate from us, all which philosophy distinguished as the NOT ME, that is, both nature and art, all other men and my own body, must be ranked under the name NATURE" (Ralph Waldo Emerson, "Nature," in *Essays and Lectures*, ed. Joel Porte [New York: Library of America, 1983], 7).

6. Henry David Thoreau, *Journal*, vol. 3, *1848–1851*, ed. Robert Sattelmeyer, Mark R. Patterson, and William Rossi, in *The Writings of Henry David Thoreau*, ser. ed. Elizabeth Hall Witherell (Princeton: Princeton University Press, 1991), 163.

7. William Blake, "The Clod and the Pebble," in *Romanticism: An Anthology*, ed. Duncan Wu (Cambridge, Mass.: Blackwell, 1995), 66.

8. Thoreau, *Journal*, 3:218.

9. According to Robert Milder, "Thoreau projects a development beyond as the soul deprived of sensible feelers begins to put forth spiritual ones. A rehearsal for death, the unconsciousness wrought by the anesthesia seems to prefigure a passage between ontological states, the future one unimaginable in substance but infinitely alluring. Initiated four days after taking the ether, Thoreau's moonlight walks of May through September seem efforts to re-enter this transition world suggestive of pre- and post-existence" (*Reimagining Thoreau* [Cambridge: Cambridge University Press, 1995], 110). However, I see the transition state as the main objective of both the ether and the moonlight experiences rather than an ontological quest for what lies beyond the transition state.

10. Thoreau, *Journal*, 3:249.

11. Ibid., 3:252.

12. Ibid., 3:259.

13. Ibid.

14. Ibid., 3:261.

15. Thoreau, *The Maine Woods*, 594.

16. Ibid., 796.

17. Ibid., 663.

18. Ibid., 671.

19. Ibid., 632.

20. Ibid.

21. Ibid., 633–34.

22. The description of the dead moose seems to anticipate Thoreau's experience of his father's death. On February 3, 1859, he writes in his Journal, "I have touched a body that was flexible and warm, yet tenantless,—warmed by what fire? When the spirit that animated some matter has left it, who else, what else, can animate it?" (Henry David Thoreau, *The Journal of Henry David Thoreau in Fourteen Volumes Bound as Two*, ed. Bradford Torrey and Francis H. Allen [1906; reprint, New York: Dover, 1962], 2:435).

23. Thoreau, *The Maine Woods*, 678. Martha Hunt, a young woman in straitened circumstances, drowned herself in the Concord River in July 1845. Hawthorne helped retrieve her body and incorporated the experience into his novel. Thoreau was in the rescue boat with Hawthorne, and I believe that the event informed his own description of dragging the female moose from the stream. See Leslie Perrin Wilson, *In History's Embrace: Past and Present in Concord, Massachusetts* (Concord, Mass.: Concord Free Public Library Corporation, 2007), 71.

24. Thoreau, *The Maine Woods*, 680.

25. Ibid., 681.

26. Ibid., 683.

27. Ibid., 684.

28. Ibid., 685.

29. Ibid., 684.

30. Ibid.

31. Thoreau's description of the murder of a pine tree may be linked to the lurid details of the prostitute Helen Jewett's 1836 murder by her lover, Richard P. Robinson. The trial transcripts were reprinted as a full front-page article in the *Concord Freeman* on June 18 of that year. My thanks to Robert Gross for the historical background.

32. Thoreau, *The Maine Woods*, 685.

33. Henry David Thoreau, *Journal*, vol. 7, *1853–1854*, ed. Nancy Craig Simmons and Ron Thomas, in *The Writings of Henry David Thoreau*, ser. ed. Elizabeth Hall Witherell (Princeton: Princeton University Press, 2009), 235.

34. Thoreau, *Maine Woods*, 638.

35. David M. Robinson draws a parallel between Thoreau's Katahdin experience and his moonlight walks (discussed previously in this chapter): "As different as these two forms of natural experience were, they had an important quality in common: they showed Thoreau the natural world from a new prospect, making the familiar seem strange . . . In both experiences, Thoreau glimpsed a natural world that was uninhabited, undomesticated, and wild" (*Natural Life: Thoreau's Worldly Transcendentalism* [Ithaca: Cornell University Press, 2004], 129–30).

36. Thoreau, *The Maine Woods*, 639.

37. Ibid.

38. Ibid., 640.

39. Ibid.

40. Ibid.

41. Ibid., 641.

42. Ibid., 640.

43. Ibid., 641–42.

44. Ibid., 645.

45. Ibid., 640.

46. Ibid., 646. Robinson notes, "This clear repudiation of his earlier anthropomorphic representations of nature is emphasized by the concentration of earth as 'matter,' and the implication that this matter is beyond the power of mind to project or control it" (*Natural Life*, 137).

47. Thoreau, *The Maine Woods*, 645.

48. Ibid., 640.

49. Ibid., 646.

50. Ibid., 730.

51. Ibid., 730–31.

52. Ibid., 731.

53. Ibid., 732.

54. John J. Kucich, "Lost in the Maine Woods: Henry David Thoreau, Joseph Nicolar, and the Penobscot World," *Concord Saunterer*, n.s., 19/20 (2011–12): 44.

55. Ibid., 45.

56. Walls, "Walking West," 21.

57. Megan Marshall, *Margaret Fuller: A New American Life* (Boston: Houghton Mifflin Harcourt, 2013), 382.

58. Henry David Thoreau, *The Correspondence of Henry David Thoreau*, ed. Walter Harding and Carl Bode (New York: New York University Press, 1958), 265.

59. Thoreau, *Journal*, 3:95. In fact, Thoreau located a scavenger named Smith Oaks on Fire Island whose dilapidated cabin contained piles of booty from shipwrecks. Oaks showed

Thoreau two trunks that had belonged to the Ossolis. One, in which Fuller was known to keep her gold watch, was empty; presumably the other held her husband's coat. See John Matteson, *The Lives of Margaret Fuller* (New York: Norton, 2012), 416–17.

60. Matteson, *Lives of Margaret Fuller*, 423.
61. Henry David Thoreau, *Journal*, vol. 4, *1851–1852*, ed. Leonard N. Neufeldt and Nancy Craig Simmons, in *The Writings of Henry David Thoreau*, ser. ed. Elizabeth Hall Witherell (Princeton: Princeton University Press, 1992), 154.
62. Thoreau, *Cape Cod*, 860.
63. Ibid., 962.
64. Ibid., 952.
65. Ibid., 853.
66. Ibid., 855.
67. Ibid., 857.
68. Ibid., 861.
69. Christopher A. Dustin, "Thoreau and the Strange Relation of Matter and Spirit," *Concord Saunterer*, n.s., 21 (2013): 59.
70. Thoreau, *Cape Cod*, 890.
71. Ibid., 918.
72. Ibid., 913–14.
73. Ibid., 933.
74. Thoreau, *Walden*, 575–76.
75. Thoreau, *Cape Cod*, 944.
76. Ibid., 940.
77. Ibid., 943.
78. Ibid., 931.
79. Ibid., 936.
80. Ibid., 900.
81. Ibid., 901–902. This passage may echo 1 Corinthians 13:12. The King James Version reads, "For now we see through a glass darkly; but then face to face: now I know in part; but then I shall know even as also I am known."
82. Thoreau, *Cape Cod*, 963.
83. Ibid., 851–52.
84. Ibid., 862.
85. Ibid., 863.
86. Ibid., 891.
87. Ibid., 893.
88. Ibid., 897.
89. Ibid., 935.
90. Dustin, "Thoreau and the Strange Relation of Matter and Spirit," 58.
91. *Walden*, 575.
92. Walls, "Walking West," 34.
93. Thoreau, *Cape Cod*, 949.
94. Dustin, "Thoreau and the Strange Relation of Matter and Spirit," 61.
95. Thoreau, *Cape Cod*, 876.
96. Ibid., 957.
97. Ibid., 868.
98. Ibid., 961.
99. Ibid., 893.
100. Ibid., 1039.
101. Walls, "Walking West," 37.
102. Thoreau, *Walden*, 579.
103. Thoreau, *Cape Cod*, 1039.

5. "As long as she cracks she holds"

Epigraph: Drew Gilpin Faust, *This Republic of Suffering: Death and the American Civil War* (New York: Knopf, 2008), xv.

1. David S. Reynolds, *John Brown, Abolitionist: The Man Who Killed Slavery, Sparked the Civil War, and Seeded Civil Rights* (New York: Knopf, 2005), 381.
2. Henry David Thoreau, *Collected Essays and Poems,* ed. Elizabeth Hall Witherell (New York: Library of America, 2001), 395.
3. Henry David Thoreau, *A Week on the Concord and Merrimack Rivers, Walden, The Maine Woods, Cape Cod,* ed. Robert F. Sayre (New York: Library of America, 1985), 336.
4. Thoreau, *Essays and Poems,* 387–88.
5. Louisa May Alcott, *Moods: A Novel* (Boston: Loring, 1864); Louisa May Alcott, Work: A Study of Experience (Boston: Roberts, 1873).
6. Rose Hawthorne Lathrop, "Thoreau and Alcott," in *Thoreau amongst Friends and Philistines and Other Thoreauviana,* ed. Dr. Samuel Arthur Jones (1903; reprint, Athens: Ohio University Press, 1982), 182–83.
7. Robert D. Richardson, Jr., *Henry Thoreau: A Life of the Mind* (Berkeley: University of California Press, 1986), 389.
8. Lawrence Buell, *The Environmental Imagination: Thoreau, Nature Writing, and the Formation of American Culture* (Cambridge: Harvard University Press, 1995), 336.
9. Sophia Thoreau, letter to Daniel Ricketson, May 20, 1962, in *Daniel Ricketson and His Friends,* ed. Anna Ricketson and Walton Ricketson (Boston: Houghton Mifflin, 1902), 141.
10. Henry David Thoreau, letter to Daniel Ricketson, February 12, 1859, in ibid., 92.
11. Richardson, Henry Thoreau, 334–36.
12. Henry David Thoreau, letter to Harrison G. O. Blake, June 27, 1855, in *The Correspondence of Henry David Thoreau,* ed. Walter Harding and Carl Bode (New York: New York University Press, 1958), 376–77.
13. William Howarth, *The Book of Concord* (New York: Viking, 1982), 63.
14. Ralph Waldo Emerson, "Thoreau," in *Essays and Poems,* ed. Joel Porte, Harold Bloom, and Paul Kane (New York: Library of America, 1996), 1009–27.
15. Thoreau, letter to Blake, June 27, 1855. Previously, I discussed how frequently Thoreau identified himself with the feminine. Here, he seems to be playing with the notion that too much writing can be dangerous, even fatal, to a woman.
16. Henry David Thoreau, letter to Harrison G. O. Blake, September 26, 1855, in *Correspondence,* 383–85.
17. Henry David Thoreau, *The Journal of Henry David Thoreau in Fourteen Volumes Bound as Two,* ed. Bradford Torrey and Francis H. Allen (1906; reprint, New York: Dover, 1962), 2:272.
18. Unless otherwise noted, all details of Thoreau's death are gleaned from Sophia Thoreau's letters to Daniel Ricketson (Ricketson and Ricketson, *Daniel Ricketson and His Friends*).
19. Mann's promising career as a naturalist and a professor ended tragically: he died of consumption at the age of twenty-four. He may have contracted it while traveling with Thoreau (Walter Harding, *The Days of Henry Thoreau: A Biography* [New York: Dover, 1962], 451).
20. Ibid., 463.
21. Ibid., 460.
22. Ibid., 456.
23. Ibid., 461.
24. Ibid., 463.
25. William Ellery Channing, *Thoreau the Poet-Naturalist, with Memorial Verses* (Boston: Goodspeed, 1902), 340.

26. Ibid., 343.

27. Mary Hosmer Brown, *Memories of Concord* (Boston: Four Seasons, 1926), 106.

28. Channing was much closer to Thoreau than Emerson was in the last dozen years of his life. According to both Alcott and Sanborn, Channing never recovered from Thoreau's death. Rather than seeing his friend's early death as a "broken task," he believed that Thoreau's death broke his survivors' tasks. In a memorial sonnet published in the *Concord Monitor* on May 10, 1862, Channing seems to counter Emerson's point of view:

> THOREAU! 't'were shame to weep above thy grave,
> Or doubtingly thy soul's far flight pursue;
> Peace and delight must there await the brave,
> And love attend the loving, wise, and true.
> Thy well-kept vows our broken aims shall mend,
> Oft as we think on thee, great-hearted friend!

29. Raymond Borst, *Henry David Thoreau: A Reference Guide, 1835–1899* (Boston: Hall, 1987), 32.

30. Ricketson and Ricketson, *Daniel Ricketson and His Friends*, 151.

31. Richard W. Fox, *Jesus in America: Personal Savior, Cultural Hero, and National Obsession* (San Francisco: HarperCollins, 2005), 240.

32. Samuel Ripley Bartlett, "Walden," *Concord Monitor*, May 17, 1862, 33–34, reprinted in *Emerson Society Quarterly* 7 (2nd quarter 1957): 42–43.

33. Harding, *Days of Henry Thoreau*, 257.

34. Sophia told Ricketson in a May 26, 1862, letter that she "liked [the Dunshee] better than his other daguerreotypes," an indication there were probably more likenesses of Thoreau that have since been lost (Ricketson and Ricketson, *Daniel Ricketson and His Friends*, 147).

35. Ibid.

36. Henry David Thoreau, *Journal*, vol. 4, *1851–1852*, ed. Leonard N. Neufeldt and Nancy Craig Simmons, in *The Writings of Henry David Thoreau*, ser. ed. Elizabeth Hall Witherell (Princeton: Princeton University Press, 1992), 176.

37. Ibid., 281–82.

38. Ibid., 434.

39. Sophia Thoreau, letter to Daniel Ricketson, May 18, 1863, in Ricketson and Ricketson, *Daniel Ricketson and His Friends*, 156.

40. Sophia Thoreau, letter to Daniel Ricketson, February 7, 1863, in ibid., 154.

41. Sophia Thoreau, letter to Daniel Ricketson, December 15, 1863, in ibid., 159.

42. W. Barksdale Maynard, *Walden Pond: A History* (New York: Oxford University Press, 2004), 158–59.

43. Franklin B. Sanborn, *Henry David Thoreau* (1882; reprint, Chelsea House, 1980), 317.

44. Sophia Thoreau, letter to Daniel Ricketson, February 2, 1863, in Ricketson and Ricketson, *Daniel Ricketson and His Friends*, 155.

45. Sophia Thoreau, letter to Daniel Ricketson, July 17, 1865, in ibid., 165–66.

46. Ibid., 166.

47. Robert D. Richardson, Jr., *Emerson: The Mind on Fire* (Berkeley: University of California Press, 1995), 548.

48. Though Emerson never uses the word stoic in his eulogy, it does appear in his laudatory obituary for Thoreau, published on May 9, 1862, in the *Boston Daily Advertiser*: "He was a man of stoic temperament, highly intellectual, of a perfect probity." My thanks to Richard Smith for alerting me to the existence of this obituary.

49. Emerson, "Thoreau," 1012.

50. Ibid., 1017.

51. Ibid., 1013.

52. Ibid., 1014.

53. Ibid., 1013.
54. Ibid., 1024–25.
55. Ibid., 1027.
56. Ibid., 1012, 1021, 1014.
57. Thoreau, *Essays and Poems,* 23.
58. Thoreau, *Journal,* ed. Torrey and Allen, 2:426.
59. Maynard, *Walden Pond,* 148.
60. Ibid., 156.
61. Thoreau is referring to a game that boys played at the end of winter—daring each other to skate out on the thinning ice. He writes near the end of *Walden,* "It affords me no satisfaction to commence to spring an arch before I have got a solid foundation. Let us not play at kittybenders. There is a solid bottom everywhere" (*Walden,* 285).
62. Franklin B. Sanborn, *The Personality of Thoreau* (Boston: Goodspeed, 1901), 69.

Index

Audrey Raden, a published poet and essayist and an English professor for a number of years in the City University of New York system, received her PhD in 2013 from the CUNY Graduate School. In 2013 she also entered New York Theological Seminary, where she is pursuing a Master of Divinity and studying to be a hospice chaplain. Though she would love to live in Concord, MA, she nevertheless lives happily in New York City with her husband, John Eiche, and their cat, Increase.